OBJECTS
IN THE
MIRROR

www.mascotbooks.com

For more information, please contact:
Mascot Books
620 Herndon Parkway #320
Herndon, VA 20170
info@mascotbooks.com

Library of Congress Control Number: 2020902452

CPSIA Code: PRV0820B
ISBN-13: 978-1-64543-408-5
ISBN: 978-1-64543-409-2 (eBook)

Printed in United States

I dedicate this book to my wife, Kirsten, and our daughters, Sophia, Adeline, Noelle, and Greta. You are my reason. Through each of you I have known perfection despite my own imperfections. I wrote this all down because I wanted you to know that.

OBJECTS IN THE MIRROR

Thoughts on a Perfect Life from an Imperfect Person

STEPHEN KELLOGG

American singer-songwriter

CONTENTS

Oh, the stories we could tell
And if this all blows up and goes to hell
I can still see us sittin' on the bed in some motel
Listenin' to the stories we could tell

—John Sebastian

I know what I am about, my love, and will take the
liberty of expressing myself accordingly.

—Charles Dickens, *The Old Curiosity Shop*

I write for only two reasons: to please myself and to
please others.

—Stephen King

AUTHOR'S NOTE

The characters in this book are real. They are all from my life, and I can't say exactly how they'll feel about me relaying my experiences. This is not a memoir, but I've left in many personal details, because in writing about important subject matters, the particulars are worth sharing. I imagine some will enjoy seeing their name in lights and others may not. In the case of positive encounters, I've left in real names; I'd like to give credit where credit is due. In other areas where the interaction was less affirmative, I've used pseudonyms. My intention is never to wound, only to share the truth as I see it. I hope that comes across.

FOREWORD

by Adam Duritz

Rock and roll is a small club of fairly strange people motivated, for some bizarre reason, to routinely vomit up their lives and feelings for everyone else's consumption. And, as Frank Turner once sang, "Some of them are just like us and some of them are dicks." Some of them are also the best people I've ever known. Stephen Kellogg falls into that last category. So, when he decided to write a book and asked me to read it, I was thrilled to find not some run-of-the-mill road life rockography, but rather a book about a guy living a truly full and revealingly human life, all expressed through the experiences, thoughts, loves, fears, and tears of my friend Stephen. Check it out.

INTRODUCTION

I had just begun my 30s when I arbitrarily picked the impossibly faraway age of 40 as the year by which I would absolutely, unequivocally have written a book. Never mind that I had moved the words "write manuscript" in my old-school daily planner from week to week and month to month for more than half a decade with no sense of irony—I was going to hit this goal. So yeah...that didn't happen.

About six months after I turned 41, I did something crazy though. I announced that my book would be out by the end of the year, and I started taking advance orders for it. There was only one problem. I hadn't written it. Oh, and I wasn't sure what I would write about either. But, hey, necessity is the mother of invention, and there is nothing like fear of failure to light a fire under your ass.

So the first reason for writing this book, which I'm only slightly embarrassed to admit, was to see if I could do it. Like

George Mallory, who when asked why he wanted to climb Mount Everest answered, "Because it's there," I wanted to see if I could write something worth reading. I had friends who had successfully added authorship to their résumés, and I wanted to join their ranks.

I started by making a list of things I might be interested in and/or qualified to talk about. Things I had accomplished. Adventures I'd been a part of. Remarkable people I had met. Mistakes I had made and been able to learn from. Mistakes I continued to make. I took stock of memories worth remembering. I mined my journals and notebooks. Had tea with creative friends and discussed life and our short stay on this planet as though it were the only thing worth discussing. It dawned on me: Maybe it *is* the only thing worth discussing.

Our use of time and the way we prioritize our existence is a reflection of who we are. I've had friends who watch hours of TV every single day say to me with a straight face that they wish they had time to read a book. I'm not judging them (OK, well, maybe a little), but knowing that we all have a different set of priorities, I began to wonder, *What could be more important than figuring out what's most important?*

Gradually, by asking myself that question, I came to the following conclusion: What we focus on while we're here matters. We matter, every last one of us. And our success, if you can call it that, will not be measured in dollars and cents but rather by the quality of our relationships and the depth of our character.

● · · · · · · · · · · · · · · · ● · · · · · · · · · · · · · · · · ●

Through some combination of good fortune and a sanguine disposition, I have, up to this moment, been living a charmed life. I realize this may make my point of view suspect to those who have not been as fortunate in their prospects, but in sharing what I'm about to share, I've tried to account for the role that luck plays in the outcome of a person's journey.

At the age of 23 I began the vocation of my dreams as a singer and songwriter, signing my first record deal with Universal in 2004. The job has taken me to more than 2,000

Through no effort of my own, I was born in the USA where, at least at the time of this writing, civil liberties remain intact and relative peace is the order of the day. Raised up from loving middle-class parents, I was educated by many intelligent and thoughtful teachers. I married my high school sweetheart, who, through some stroke of divinity, still seems to like me quite a bit after 26 years; we have four daughters, whom I live to impress. That may not be the sexiest reason for trying to be a better person, but it is mine.

stages in 21 countries. I've met many of my heroes along the way and made enduring friendships that I treasure. I've watched John Daly drive a golf ball off of his brother's mouth, been written up in *Rolling Stone*, played at Red Rocks and The Greek Theater. I've landed on an aircraft carrier, had my work nominated for a Grammy, and seen the inside of the Oval Office. I've also spent the night on the side of the road, inadvertently plagiarized Paul Simon, completely blown it on national TV, and been chased out of a club by an angry mob. I've almost run out of money on more than one occasion. I wouldn't trade any of it.

As you'll see throughout these pages, I'm a highly flawed individual, not the least of which is as a writer. I thought it would be much easier to transition from my role as on-stage storyteller to solitary author. I had grand visions of writing a book that would be all-encompassing, speaking to every single person who read it. It turned out to be a lot more difficult than I thought it'd be, which I guess could also be said of life.

After several frustrating drafts and attempts to hear my own voice coming through on the page, I had another major epiphany: It's much easier to be yourself than somebody you are not. People listen to my music and what I have to say not because I'm always right or some kind of guru, but rather because I relish my transparency. I'm comfortable in my own skin and what you see is what you get. I'd rather relate deeply to one person than on a surface level to many people.

I will never be the poster boy for any of the topics included herein, so instead of trying to cover all aspects of every subject, I've decided to talk about what it's like to screw up on a daily basis and be OK with that. To be someone who believes the future *might* be better than the past if we work hard at it, a melancholy optimist in the middle of a perfectly imperfect life. Let me talk about what it's like to be me.

● · · · · · · · · · · · · · · · · · ● · · · · · · · · · · · · · · · · ●

You'll notice there are lyrics at the beginning of each chapter. These are the songs from the album I made while writing this book. While it's not necessary to have the music to get something out of the text or vice versa, you can consider them companion pieces—one more glimpse into the subject matter.

In a lot of ways these essays are written like songs: You take from them what resonates. Whatever it is that you need at this moment. I want to be clear that this is not an instruction manual. The point is not to say, "Live as I do," but rather, "Here's what I have found."

While I may have initially wanted to write a book to prove something to myself, one of those things we learn as we get older is that self-interest can only take us so far. This is for me *and* for you. These are stories without any clear good guys or bad guys. Instead, in each of these vignettes you will find dysfunctional humans trying to do their best and bouncing off each other in the process.

●·················●·················●

In the spaces of our long days and fast years, there will be marriages to attend to, kids to raise, heroes to worship, and aging parents to consider. Friends will come and go like the seasons. We'll have ample opportunity to make mistakes in all these relationships, and if we're lucky, we'll have a chance to get it right sometimes too. We'll discover on our own schedule the essential components of a life well lived: the way we spend our time; our health; our work; our sense of humor; our integrity; our ability to forgive; and a meaningful legacy. These are what I call *objects in the mirror.* The contents of our wonderfully imperfect lives rushing past us.

So often we get focused on trying to do things our way, which we feel is the correct way, and in striving for a perfection that does not exist, it's easy to end up missing not just the moment but the point. Putting together this book was no exception. In the end, though, I preferred to share what was on my mind, so I took a swing.

PART ONE

RELATIONSHIPS

LOVE OF MY LIFE

At any time, in any space
I'm sure I would have recognized your face
A vision like Helen of Troy
You came to me when I was still a boy
It was you I had to find
And I could have found you blind

Of all of the best memories that live in my head
It's you in those blue jeans on the day that we met
I knew right then we would be friends
You're the love of my life

Your mom in heaven looking down
I think she knew it when she met me and she helped you figure out
Of all those guys knocking on your door
There would never be one who'd love you more

Of all of the best memories that live in my head
It's you in those blue jeans on the day that we met
I knew right then we would be friends
You're the love of my life

This is a simple song about simple things
A boy and a girl, and a wedding ring
Saying it simple doesn't make it mean less
Oh, from those blue jeans, right to that wedding dress...
You're the love of my life

CHAPTER 1
MARRIAGE

I get asked about marriage a lot. People will come up to me and say, "How do you guys do it with you being away so much?" Before I can crack a joke that phone sex has never been easier, they'll tell me that long-distance relationships are hard and that my wife must be a "trooper." I'm always tempted to say, "And your question was?" But they aren't really looking for an answer. More often than not, these folks are simply seeking solidarity with the notion that marriage is difficult. To say otherwise will make you no friends in the married community. Furthermore, the moniker of a good marriage is likely to spark more resentment than interest, while learning about a bad marriage always elicits a knowing nod. We're more fascinated with relationships that go sideways because without conflict there's no real story. I get it.

It's not that I can't relate. Believe me there is *plenty* of conflict in my own marriage, and when I meet a couple that appears to get along perfectly, I immediately cross them off my list of people I ever want to see again. Truly the stereotype that marriage is hard does have foundational accuracy—about half end in divorce—but I also think it can be kind of a cop out if we accept it as though we were passive participants with no ability to affect the end result.

If we decide to get married and stay married (some do not and that's fine), it is one of the most monumental decisions we're ever going to make. Yet somehow we don't think twice about undertaking it with no formal training whatsoever. We rely on our gut to provide us with all the answers. Even though we'd never attempt to fly a plane or perform surgery with no experience, we assume that the complex inner workings of a long-term relationship are something we can just kind of pick up without too much trouble. In lieu of real-life role models to emulate, we turn to truncated pop culture examples of what true love supposedly looks like. We're stuck relying on fanciful shows like

The Bachelor and gossip magazines like *In Touch Weekly* to show us the way. No wonder it doesn't pan out for a lot of us. We're flying blind.

Why? What's getting in the way of discovering exactly what it takes to be part of a marriage that has real synergy? I can't say for sure, but I do know that this particular area of my life has always clicked, so with no science to back me up and no guarantee that I'm correct, here's an abridgment of what has worked for me.

Number one: Marry a best friend. Not someone you need to make excuses or put on a show for, but someone whom you love to hang out with. If that sounds like a platitude, I can find a more complex way to say it, but I'd rather not. You can't marry for appearances. It takes magnetism to draw us in, but chemistry's a fickle mistress, and someday everyone, including you, is going to look a little less new.

Number two: *Learn what your partner needs and what you need, and then—you guessed it—try to meet those needs.* If the first step is picking the right car, consider this the part where we bring it in for regular oil changes. You can start by asking your spouse what's important to them and telling them what's important to you. This would be called communication. It's revolutionary, but it just might work!

Lastly, make an effort. Remember that first date? Try to

act that way as opposed to the stressed out, crabby version of yourself that you fear you have become. You're going to be together for some time, and if you start making a laundry list of everything your husband or wife has ever said or done that wasn't cool, well that's not going to be very much fun is it? No, it's not.

So in theory, you have here the foundation for a solid matrimony, but as I mentioned in the introduction, I'm no angel. Allow me to elaborate.

THE CONFLICT

"You're such a dick," she said to me.

I followed her into the next room and asked her point blank, "You think I'm a dick or you think I'm just acting like a dick?"

"I'm not sure I understand the distinction."

Indignant, I protested. "Well, there's a big difference. If you think I'm a dick, that's a terrible thing. If you think I'm just *acting* like a dick, that seems like something well within the marital agreement."

Even the way I was presenting the question was clearly a dick move, but I couldn't help myself. What's the saying?

When you find yourself in a hole, the first step is to stop digging? Not me. I bring in a backhoe and go for a full excavation. But we were fighting, or "arguing" if that makes you more comfortable, and this game of semantics struck me as the best available move at the time. If I had to talk to someone like me, I'd probably want to vaporize them with my eyes, but then again, maybe I had a point.

"I guess you're just acting like one," she said, and although she didn't smile, I thought I detected the slightest hint of amusement in her tone. I knew we could fix it, and I said as much. She looked dubious.

THE LOVE STORY

I loved her the moment I saw her. It was as though I had been trying to locate her since before I was born. *Ah, there she is,* my subconscious seemed to say. It was the second weekend of junior year in high school, and I had arrived with my friend Henry at the semester's first "mixer." We entered the cafeteria where the dance was already underway, and my eyes were immediately drawn to a small group of unfamiliar young ladies. They were surrounded by boys, and it occurred to me that she was out of my league.

She stood out, even in the company of beautiful girls. A stunner in her blue jean shorts, with a face and figure that were nothing short of miraculous, it's a wonder I didn't spontaneously combust on the spot. If I'd had any idea how important it was that I succeed in my quest to win the heart of Kirsten Caffrey, whose name I did not yet know, I'm sure I would have buckled under the pressure. Luckily, I had no clue what the stakes were.

Kirsten and her friends came from the Convent of Sacred Heart in Greenwich, CT. Her graduating class was about 25 students. I imagine if she had gone to a bigger school where there were more "options," that I wouldn't be writing this story. But she didn't, and I am, so there.

I myself was a student at the all-male Jesuit high school Fairfield Prep, where more than a few of my classmates spent their weekends drinking 40-ounce bottles of malt liquor, trying to hook up with the opposite sex, and doing their best to stay off their parents' radar. The fact that we never had the slightest grasp of what happened in the movies we were purportedly always going to see should have been a dead giveaway that we were not being entirely truthful as to our whereabouts. *Schindler's List* came out around that time, and I can still remember offering up "Oh, it was really cool" as a response to my parents' question "How was the movie?"

I disliked high school, but somehow I ended up being the class president for all four years. I suppose that suggests a certain level of popularity, but it wasn't something I felt. For most of the evening at that mixer, I couldn't gin up the courage to talk to my future wife, never mind imagine that someday, years from now, she'd be, correctly, calling me a dick. My odds of even meeting her were dwindling.

I had ignored Kirsten and her pretty friends all night, and the dance was over when music saved the day for the first (and not the last) time. From right behind me came six of the sweetest words I'd ever heard uttered before or since, "Hey, aren't you in Silent Treatment?" Huzzah! Silent Treatment was my high school heavy metal band, and as luck would have it, one of her pals had seen me play over the summer.

The window of opportunity upon me, I pulled a baller move that surprises me as much now as it did then and told her my plans to become a professional rock 'n' roll singer. Aside from maybe John Mayer (also from Fairfield), who even does that? I had never in my life exerted that kind of certainty, but later that same evening I found myself going for it again when I told my best friend's parents that I had "Just met the girl I was going to marry." I was 15 years old and did not have Kirsten's number or any way of contacting her, but on that particular night in the fall of 1992, I was calling the shots like Babe Ruth.

THE MARRIAGE

You're probably wondering when I get to the part where I teach you all my tricks for an easy union, free of animosity and filled with daily bliss. That section's coming now.

People marry for all kinds of reasons. We marry because we don't want to be alone. We marry for lust. We marry for acceptance and validation. Because it looks good on paper. We marry for financial stability, someone to help us with all these bills. We marry because it's what we think we are supposed to do. We want to experience a wedding or start building a family. We marry to check a box, thinking this part of our life will be "all figured out." Ha! We meet someone and try to mold them into that which we wish them to be. We marry for all these reasons and a thousand more. I certainly did. But I believe now that there is only one real reason a couple should ever take vows: because you've met your best friend and it's impossible to imagine life without each other.

I know this might seem like an oversimplification, but

I'm not trying to be cute here. Sometimes we think we've met *the one*, and we turn out to be wrong. It happens. We misjudge. People change. People grow apart. But if we don't start with deep, profound friendship, we're pretty well screwed from the outset. I've toured with guys over the years who refused to share with their girlfriends or wives anything fun that happened because they were afraid it would make them jealous. I never understood that. Shouldn't a best friend want you to be happy? Isn't that the whole idea of a best friend? To find somebody we can be ourselves around without having to do any acting. Being able to sleep with one of these people might just be the most amazing fringe benefit of all time, but if it interferes with the friendship, they're probably not marriage material.

THE WEDDING

A wedding is not a marriage. It's important not to mistake the two, and yet, a lot of us do. In most cases—not all— it's a celebration designed to reflect the love of the couple. But how often does that happen? We've all got a whack job uncle or at least a drunken friend who is bound to ruin the pictures or make a speech that no one asked them to. Some of the most fun weddings I've been to never should have happened. A number of my divorced friends confess that they knew "even on their wedding day" that it wasn't right. *Well, why the hell didn't you say something? And while we're on the subject, can I have back the All-Clad stainless-steel pots I bought you?*

I proposed to Kirsten before I was sure that marriage was something I was enough of an adult to do. At 24 it was hard to conceive of myself as the man of the house. The first time we slept at my in-laws after getting married, I half expected to awake to my father-in-law standing over me with a bat. I had not, after all, asked his permission to marry his daughter. Instead I told him of my intentions to propose and expressed that I would "like his blessing." *Your vote would be a real cherry on top, sir, but I'm doing this either way.* Small distinction, but I wasn't taking any chances. That's the crazy thing about marriage. It just makes it so official. It says to the world, "I've made my choice; my one selection. You weren't born in my family, but I like you so much I want you to be a part of my family."

Our wedding was a blur. I insisted to my future mother-in-law that she was being a tyrant for telling *me*, a musician, that we should hire the band *she* had found. I pretended to be considering a jazz trio and acted quite put-upon for a guy who wasn't paying for a nickel of the party. We went with her recommendation but not without my being a sourpuss. I've since attended no less than 50 weddings, and I must confess, I have never heard a better wedding band. Despite my taciturn approach to the whole thing, at the end of it I got to call myself a husband, and that's not nothing.

THE MARRIAGE, PART TWO

Around the time Kirsten and I got hitched, my mother invited a number of married friends to her beach house and asked them all to give us a piece of advice. We strolled up and down the shore with each couple, listening to their guidance, and we carried with us a symbolic walking stick, though I wish it had been a bottle of booze 'cause that might have eased some of the awkwardness of having my parents' friends tell us to be "generous with our bodies." They probably weren't much older than I am now, and their point was a good one, but still, you understand...it was a lot to process.

Listening came up an awful lot (as it should have). Trust, that was a big one. Giving your heart freely and without reservation. Fidelity was mentioned, though a person who doesn't comprehend that cheating in a relationship is waiving all rights to further comment should probably not be getting married in the first place.

Of all the lessons offered on the beach that day, there was one piece of advice that always stayed with me: Learn each other's needs and attend to them graciously. This may be the most important thing I'm going to say on this particular topic, so for the sake of emphasis, allow me to repeat myself by stating that the way we support each other will most likely dictate how satisfied we are in our marriages. It starts with understanding what is needed.

What fundamental things did I need to be happy? *Intellectual stimulation, physical touch, and plenty of spontaneity.* And what would be essential to Kirsten's sense of well-being? *Exercise, travel, and a positive atmosphere to live in.* These things kept our lights on. Without them, the spark could go out.

We aren't always going to know exactly what we need, but usually if we give it some thought, we can figure it out. Once we do (and this step is big), it's up to us to make it known. It doesn't matter whether we write it or say it so long as we find a way to share it that isn't just, "If you loved me, you'd know." Too often, we are afraid to ask for what we want—it makes us too vulnerable—and that fear of asking for what one needs puts the responsibility on our partner to magically fathom it, which is, of course, entirely unfair. Life is much too short for that kind of guesswork. And if you're lucky enough to learn what illuminates the love of your life... well then...you know what has to be done.

THE LOVE STORY, PART TWO

Everyone in my orbit knows the backstory of how I fell for Kirsten. But if you're asking precisely when she decided to love me back, that's harder to pinpoint. I've got the date identified as on or around September 3, 1998. If you're crunching the numbers, that's about six years after we first met. Not exactly love at first sight. Especially when you consider that we dated almost all that time.

While I can't be sure of the exact moment, I'm not basing my guesstimate on pure fiction. A few summers ago, we were having dinner with a group of friends when we started swapping accounts of how we first fell in love with our spouses. Even couples that don't get along all that well enjoy telling the tale of how they got together. "We're complete opposites" one might say, and then take a generous amount of time describing that he likes olives and she does not. Or detailing how she's always cold and he's always hot. To be sure, it can be interesting to hear how people met, it just depends on how much you like them and how high your tolerance for details is.

When it was our turn to share, I led with the story of the dance. I felt noble for having chosen correctly at such a young age, though really that's kind of like being proud of winning the lottery. Ya got lucky, kid, that's all. Then Kirsten spoke up, "I guess for me it must have been on that cross-country trip we took after we graduated college." To the others this was a reasonable answer, but I couldn't wrap my head around the arithmetic. Assuming she didn't fall in love with me on the first day of said trip and that it fell somewhere in the middle of our journey, that puts her deciding that she loved me too at about 2,190 days into our courtship.

Think about that for a second. What one person knows immediately, another could actually wake up every day for 2,190 days and say, "I'm not sure yet. Maybe this is my guy, or maybe not." Then on the 2,191st day they get out of bed and proclaim, "This *is* someone I love."

I pointed this out. Everyone looked a little uncomfortable. My wife laughed and said, "Better late than never."

THE CONFLICT REVISITED

She was not laughing now though. In fact, quite the opposite. I can't remember what the disagreement was about, but I know I made her cry—never a good thing. Made doubly problematic by the fact that she doesn't often cry. I cry. She's rather stoic and everyone in the family, including me, is impressed by it. While my kids find Prince Harry shedding tears at his wedding to be endearing, if I emote at even the saddest, most heart-wrenching movie—*P.S. I Love You,* for instance—I'm met with a look from my toddler that says, "You're pathetic." But crying because you feel sadness or empathy versus crying because someone has been an asshole to you are altogether different animals. I'm guessing this was a case of the latter, because when Kirsten leveled the now-famous "you're such a dick" insult at me, there was a screen door that slammed, a kitchen that was stormed out of, and plenty of tears.

THE MARRIAGE, PART THREE

As with any relationship, the best ones occur when we welcome the whole of the person, warts and all. This is where making an effort comes into play. All manner of things can put pressure on a marriage (kids, health, work, money, etc.), and I'll be covering most of them in this book, but suffice it to say, yes, there will be legitimate stress that will have to be endured as a team. For this reason, we need to not blame one another for every little misfortune that comes our way. That book that sold a gazillion copies...*Don't Sweat the Small Stuff*? That's the idea.

In a marriage, all of our idiosyncrasies are on display and will be every day until "death do us part." It's impossible to hide from someone who sees us all the time, and it doesn't pay to be mad at each other just because we know where the bones are buried. Eventually we will discover all the buttons to push, for better or worse. The beauty in a marriage comes from not pushing the ones that cause pain. We don't want to trade the memory of the first date for the projection of the next annoyance. Maybe we've heard each other's stories a thousand times, but that doesn't mean they aren't worth hearing again. (Full disclosure: This is a shameless plug for the fact that my wife has heard me tell the "you're such a dick" yarn so many times that I think she might really be ready to kill me.)

Before I tell you how the big fracas with Kirsten and I played out, I'm going to give you one last example that demonstrates my point about making an effort. I'm pulling this hypothetical anecdote out of the clear blue sky.

Let's say you're married to the most gorgeous woman you can imagine. You've spent a romantic night on the town, during which you've had a chance to reconnect and reaffirm your support of each other. What's more, she wore her high heels and low-cut blouse. When you get home brimming with excitement, she slips upstairs, where you find her, less than three minutes later, not only in her pajamas, but *flossing in bed*. Now let's suppose this is a pattern you have come to know well and protested for some years, when one day, without warning, you decide to accept it and cease all objections. Instead you become like a dental hygienist assisting the process. You bring the Oral-B to her bedside table, hand her a tissue, and put her heels in the closet. You kiss her on the forehead and chuckle as you think to yourself, *Hottest girl in the world, and she flosses in bed.*

This is, of course, a speculative situation and not about my own lovely wife. But, you see, the problem in this scenario is not the act of practicing oral hygiene in a space meant for other things (a deed that, although somewhat curious, hurts no one), but rather it's the desire of the husband to change who his wife fundamentally is, *a bed flosser.*

That selfsame bed flosser was now standing in our kitchen waiting for me to stop arguing in circles and being such a smart-ass.

THE CONFLICT REVISITED...AGAIN

"I'm not sure how we got here." Finally, some nonconfrontational words escape from my mouth. I heard them as though I were an outside observer listening in on our conversation.

"You're acting crazy," she said.

"I feel crazy. I feel terrible. I feel like...," I hesitated. The resolution was right there in front of me if only I could will myself onto the high road. I said nothing. Her face softened just a little, but it was unlikely to stay that way forever, and I knew I had better find a way to make amends. I was still so annoyed though. And I had every right to be annoyed about...what was I annoyed about again? Damn. I couldn't seem to remember. This is normally a good indicator that it's time to knock it off. I had to hand it to her for taking it all in stride, for loving me in the first place.

"I'm not in the business of making you unhappy. I'm sorry for that. I'm also sorry for being so emotional. I know this isn't how you would have had it go down either." I take her hand. I raise my eyebrows as if to say, "Can you believe all this?" She lets out a sigh, and we hug.

THE MARRIAGE, PART FOUR

Every marriage has a love story, a wedding, inevitable conflict, and an end. What we do between the beginning of the love story and the end makes all the difference. The world will tear us down. We don't much need our marriages to do that. If we've got someone we fancy and we learn how to communicate the things that matter to each other, then all that's left to do is care enough to respond to those needs.

My grandparents were married for 57 years. That used to seem like an eternity to me, until I married Kirsten. I guess that's how it is when you find the right partner. I walk through this life alone and so does she, but it's nice to stand next to each other. She remains the person I most want to talk to about everything. Nothing is real until I've told her. She is my best friend, the object of my fantasy, and she flosses in bed.

I am her husband. I manage to remember to ask her what her dreams are every couple of years, and at this point I know that growing old together is definitely one of them.

I have also learned that she needs to get outside for fresh air even on days when I do not, so on occasion I suggest she take time for herself. Sometimes I even do it without expecting praise for having been considerate. Men! I work to keep her love that took me 2,190 days to earn, but if I'm completely honest, it's not that much work. It's easy most of the time.

I am not a dick, but sometimes I act like one.

I WILL ALWAYS HAVE YOUR BACK

Nighttime takes what the nighttime wants
Above the clouds there is always sun
In the darkness there's no guarantee
Do you believe in what you can't see?
Late at night I see your face...

There is nothing you could do
To make me ever forget you
If we all are passing through
I've got your back and you've got mine too
I will always have your back

It's always hard when you realize
No one here's getting out alive
I look around at my friends tonight
And in this moment it's all alright
I don't want to leave this place

There is nothing you could do
To make me ever forget you
If we're all just passing through
I've got your back and you've got mine too
I will always have your back

CHAPTER 2
FRIENDS

Friends, the family we choose. Consider for a moment, how many friends you have. How many have you had in your lifetime? It's a bit overwhelming to contemplate. Especially when you think of all the different types of friends there are. Old friends. New friends. Friends of convenience. High-maintenance friends. Frenemies. Pals you adore but can only take in small doses. Those you might not see for years but are able to pick up right where you left off with—love those.

One of my favorite types is the confidant who can tell it to you like it is. My buddy Jerry can criticize my business decisions in a way that if any other person on the planet said the same thing to me, I'd bite their head off. With him I usually just say thanks. He has a way about him that says, *I love you, but you're wrong,* and because his manner indicates his love first and foremost, it doesn't even matter if he's right or wrong himself.

Go ahead, try and remember every friend you've ever made. If that's too hard, how many best friends have you had? For my part, I count 15. I'm in touch with nine of them but only close with four. I'm fortunate in that I have lots of what one would call "friends," but most days I still feel a bit isolated. I recognize, though, that there's a difference between feeling like you have no one to call and actually not having anyone to call. One is kind of a bummer, and the other is a matter of utter despair. I've been disappointed by friendship but, thankfully, never broken by it. Although I'm sure there are those who would surprise me by rising to the occasion if I needed them, I know I'm not the only one out there wondering, *Who truly cares about me?*

Here's what I've learned about friendship.

All friends are not created equal. Some are super important and really committed to their role; some are enjoyably casual about the whole thing, while still others are incidental and indifferent to the relationship (and often our feelings). Being able to distinguish the good from the bad is one of the most liberating exercises on the planet. If you've never made room for new amazing friendships by quietly and without fanfare crossing off toxic (yes, friends can be toxic) people from your list, I highly recommend it. And hanging on to a good friend is just as vital.

I've also learned that occasionally friendships end. Not out of malice. Not because we want to drift apart, but because it's natural to do so. Maintaining relationships takes lots of time and effort, and sometimes, as much as we like each other, we don't have it in us to make room for either. They can't all get the same attention, and so, over time, we might outgrow a friend or simply watch them fade away.

Lastly, when it comes to quantity vs. quality, we should always choose quality. It only takes one other person to not be alone. A single good companion is worth a thousand so-so ones. Being friends with everyone is exhausting and best left to politicians.

There isn't anyone who needs me to explain why friendships are so important. That's understood. Someone to hang with. Someone to laugh with. Someone to cry with. It makes sense. But even if we have these people in our life, is there no room for improvement in the kind of friend that we are to others? Of course there is, so read on...

THE GOOD ONES

It's much easier to tell who your real friends are when life is kicking your ass. That's when the best people around you stand up to help, to stick their neck out for you, sometimes just to be with you. On most occasions it's all we really need to weather the storm. A sense that someone has our back. Good friends do this even when it's inconvenient for them.

My daughter was getting harassed one day on the playground, when her sister approached and called the boy picking on her a "dick" (it must run in the family). I had never heard my kids use profanity, and, given that they were all in elementary school at the time, I suppose I should have told her that's not how we talk to people, but instead I found myself admiring her. She was standing with her sibling at her own peril. It was pretty badass. I considered who in my life would do the same.

Which is not to suggest that my friends haven't supported me. On the contrary, they've helped me move in hundred-degree heat, loaned me guitars when mine got stolen, watched my cat when I traveled, performed at my kids' birthday parties, and even climbed high ladders to change light bulbs when they were as afraid of heights as I was (that was a particularly fun one, having hung two floodlights successfully, Bobby Pagel and I celebrated like a couple sailors on shore leave).

On another occasion, I tried to coax my kids into dealing with some vermin in our basement. I handed a broom to the littlest one and implored them, "Come on, guys, you can do this!" They weren't to be persuaded, though, and my neighbor Dave had to come to our rescue. Luckily, he appreciated my cowardice as much as I did his bravery. He pretended not to notice as I high-stepped my way past the removal of our unwelcome guest.

My pals have done it all, and I love them for it, but it's when you're humbled that you really experience the weight of a true friend. Those times when life is *hard*.

The day of Kirsten's miscarriage comes to mind. We had been through two successful pregnancies, and it hadn't even occurred to us that these things don't always work out. We walked into the doctor's office with big goofy smiles and left less than an hour later in tears. I remember feeling quite stupid for some reason. Embarrassed. It seemed like every-one who hadn't gotten around to congratulating us chose that day to reach out. I had no idea what to say. I didn't want anyone else to feel as bad as we did, so we hid out in our house and didn't answer the phone.

That's when my cousin Jessica and her husband, Jesse,

arrived. They walked into our kitchen, gave us both a bear hug, and set to work fixing us a meal. For a while I think we just sat there. Kirsten and I always say grace before eating but not that night. Didn't have it in us. Couldn't find the words. But then Jessica could: "I'm thankful for our friendship, our health, and *your* two daughters." Somehow, she flipped the switch we couldn't seem to find, and because of that, it wasn't as dark.

•••••••••••••••••••••••••••••

Good friends appreciate our sense of humor. Nothing makes me happier than someone who enjoys my jokes. I'm like a kitten in the sun. And it's not that I'm especially funny; it's just that I welcome those who aren't above a courtesy laugh when a valiant attempt has been made. If you've ever scratched the record by making a comment that you, but no one else, thought was humorous, you know what I'm talking about. Good friends just *get* you.

On tour we spend a lot of time in the van or bus or plane or car or dressing room; things get silly. Jason "Shady" Katz has been a part of my crew for almost 20 years. We could have laughs at a funeral and probably will, so long as it's not one of us that has died. He and I like to do voices. There's the *Southern Gentleman* who is anything but a gentleman; the *Russian Operative* who is planning to use espionage to bolster flagging ticket sales; and the *Ever-Present Omniscient Narrator* whose commentary on all hapless events makes everything a little clearer; you know, just your garden-variety anti-heroes. I'm not sure if these are as funny as we think they are, and I'll be honest, they may not be totally appropriate, but I enjoy having them in my life, and they've gotten us through a lot of late-night drives.

●··············●···············●

Good friends also listen. Maybe that's why pets make such good companions. They allow us to express ourselves without comment or judgment. They never roll their eyes. No one's cat or dog or lizard has ever gotten sick of hearing them pour their heart out. With people, it's a little more complex. It's easy to want to fix each other. I'm guilty of that. But if there is one thing I have learned growing up in a houseful of women and now living with a wife and four daughters, it's that sometimes you just need to shut up and listen. It's the whole seek-to-understand-before-we-seek-to-be-understood thing.

I know I'm talking way too much when my wife starts to fall asleep while I'm answering a question that *she* asked *me*.

Still, she's one of the best listeners I know. She has a knack for hearing what's being said and giving her full attention to the conversation. (And is there anything more irritating than sharing what's on your mind with someone who is distracted? As if you're not going to know that they're checking their email when they say "that's great" after you've told them you're depressed.) If I have a problem, I can usually find a solution by just opening up to Kirsten. Sometimes she won't even have responded, and I'll find myself saying, "Wow, I feel so much better. Thanks for the talk."

● ················· ● ················· ●

Good friends like us just the way we are. They're safe to be around. Like home. They accept us unconditionally. I feel that way about my friends the McHughs. I'm close with the whole family. Jeff (the dad) is the reason I got into performing. After failing to make the basketball team for three consecutive years, he suggested I try out for the school play he was directing. Molly (the younger daughter) came to see *Oklahoma* and had a crush on the guy playing Ali Hakim (me), which prompted her brother Ian (the son) to invite yours truly to join his rock band, Silent Treatment. In addition to starting me on a path toward my future career, this also led to lots of little co-ed sleepover parties that Patty (the mom) and Bridget (the elder daughter) did their level best to disrupt—unsuccessfully, I might add.

It's been years since I slept over at the McHughs' house, but I still sometimes show up at the back porch late night to see if anyone's awake and game for a chat. They usually are. Now that texting exists, I suppose it would be a hell of a lot less startling if I were to announce my visits, but they don't seem to mind. There isn't a single thing I would alter about any of them. In my book, that's about the highest compliment you can pay a friend.

I am, however, nothing if not painfully self-aware, and I suspect there are a few characteristics of my own personality that folks might like to modify. Let me see if I can think of any...

I'm emotional. I overeat. I can't keep a secret. I'm terrible with technology. I'm OCD. I don't love having houseguests. I'm a hypochondriac. I'm a workaholic. Sometimes I raise my voice. I'm not fiscally conservative. I am socially liberal. I'm also a man's man. I'm impatient in the workplace. I hate practicing music. I'm jealous. I cry easily. I'm impulsive. I find willful ignorance infuriating and am the worst at hiding it. I'm an introvert. I brush my teeth half-heartedly. I strongly dislike Halloween and awards ceremonies. I shed. I have bad skin. I wear nothing but my underwear for at least a portion of every day regardless of where I am, what I'm doing, or whom I'm doing it with.

So, yeah, I am aware I'm not perfect. But my real friends know this, and they like me anyway. That's the idea.

●················●················●

Good friends don't talk behind our back—at least not much. OK, look, we all say things about each other once in a while. How can we not? Without question, people—even friends— can be annoying. There has to be room in the relationship for some dissent. We can't be expected to agree about every-thing. So on occasion we vent to third parties in the hopes of feeling better, or at least more "right," which is what we're really looking for when we tell our tale of woe to others. The problem is that it's possible to fall into a pattern of pouring gasoline on the fire by never bringing our issues directly to those with whom we have the disconnect.

And it's gotten harder than ever to stay out of the fray. With today's political climate, avoiding full on loggerheads, even with our good buddies, is a victory unto itself. To say nothing of what can happen should we make a misstep on social media. Suddenly we are called to share and comment on everything. The world demands we choose sides and create a window into our personal lives. If we try to avoid the new normal, we may be shunned. Folks will wonder why we didn't know it was their birthday or respond to an Evite. Something as simple as failing to like a friend's Facebook post can warrant drawing lines in the sand. Feelings get hurt easily. And there is nothing like wounded pride to invoke gossip. Either we learn how to control the medium, or the medium controls us.

It's easy to seek refuge in a bit of good old-fashioned commiseration. But if it's the rule and not the exception, something is off. This is where we go back to the example of our pets. They never talk behind anyone's back and have no ulterior motives. When we take our grievances everywhere but where they belong, we erode real camaraderie. The relationship is guaranteed to suffer. And if we're doing it to others, there is a good chance they're doing it to us. That's usually a pretty clear sign that it's time to move on.

WHEN FRIENDSHIPS END

A few months ago, I pulled an "Irish Goodbye" at a gathering of fellow artists. For those of you not familiar with the phrase, this is when you slip out the back without saying that you're leaving. I glanced around the room and realized that, although I had known many of those in attendance for years, they felt like strangers to me. So I left. If anyone noticed or cared, they didn't say anything about it. And nothing at all was wrong. I wasn't mad or unhappy; I just didn't feel a connection to the evening or the people who were there.

However it may seem, the Irish Goodbye is not always a result of an unpleasant situation. If you're thinking about somebody who ghosted out on your Super Bowl party, don't assume it's a bad thing. On the bright side, they didn't kill the vibe by making a big to-do of their exit. The same can be said when we let go of a friendship that has run its course. At least we didn't kill the vibe.

●················●················●

In the spring of 2008, I spent every day for a month hanging out with George Thorogood and the Destroyers. George was funny and thoughtful. He loved old country songs and history books. We ate a lot of meals together and would talk about our families while sipping seltzer. In short, nothing about him was "Bad To The Bone." I loved passing time with George.

At the conclusion of every tour, though, there is a moment when you realize it's about to end. The close company you've been keeping for weeks will no longer be around when you get back to your other more domestic routines at home. The inside jokes won't make as much sense when next you meet, if in fact you ever meet again. For first-timers this can be a harsh reality, bound to elicit the blues. It's a shock to discover that the person whose snoring has been driving you nuts for days has endeared himself to you in such a way that you can now scarcely imagine falling asleep without him in earshot. But once you've been through it a few times, you realize how natural it is to splinter off in different directions.

On the last night of the Thorogood tour, there was a note in my dressing room when I got off stage. Next to the note was George's bracelet made from bullets. I didn't see him leave that night, and I've never seen him since, but that doesn't mean we weren't friends.

● ················· ● ················· ●

Before I knew what I know now, I'm sure I thought all my friendships would last forever. Boyhood pals would segue into college friends, and all those people at my wedding would be there with us at our golden anniversary. My former bandmates, acquaintances, and neighbors would be there too—all one big happy faux family. We had dreamed things together. That had to count for something. And it did. But we had also dreamed things apart.

In most cases the relationships didn't fracture. They simply went away. Distance forms with the passage of time. On the occasions where the separation was more intentional, it was usually because one person was hanging on a little tighter than the other, and like a tooth in need of extraction, it was simply time to pull the plug on it. Remember, friendship shouldn't hurt that much—a little maybe, but not too much. No use trying to be simpatico with someone who doesn't share your ardor.

QUALITY VS. QUANTITY

The parties we aren't invited to are often the ones we end up thinking about the most. I can still remember, at the end of sixth grade, a boy having a class-wide gathering where only three kids were not invited. I'll give you one guess as to who was not on that guest list. That's right: your trusty author. WTF. I mean, if you're having a small get-together, sure invite whomever you want. But a class-wide shindig with all the 10-year-olds in town minus this guy? Go jump in a lake.

It turned out not to be as much of a deal for me as it might have been because Chris Tar, who *was* invited to the big soiree, told me he planned to skip it if I wasn't going to be there. And that made me feel amazing.

We've all been left out at some point in our life, and it stings. We want to be liked, and the omission would indicate otherwise. But I learned a long time ago that a friend who makes you keep on auditioning for his or her friendship is no friend at all. No one wants to be around people who make them feel self-conscious. We can do that on our own without any help from others. We want to feel valued by our friends, as though they're as lucky to have us as we are to have them.

All the same, I do sometimes still catch myself doing the dance. It doesn't go away just because we grow up and become adults. On Instagram it looks like everyone is having a great time, all the time, with everybody else. And when it comes to my professional life, my FOMO is legendary. But then again, no one is posting pictures of their underattended concerts, bad hair days, or moments of self-doubt. I know this, but it doesn't always help.

What if, instead of trying to be "besties" with lots of people, we focused only on the ones who make us happy?

For real happy. Like, here-are-two-front-row-tickets-to-Def-Leppard happy. Like, you-take-the-last-bite-of-ice-cream-cause-I-know-it's-your-favorite happy. Would that whittle down the list considerably? Sure. But does that matter if there is a person that genuinely wants to join us for Def Leppard and ice cream?

We don't need an army. All we really require is someone who doesn't need us to be more, or less, than we already are.

BEING A FRIEND

At various times in my life I've had the chance to be a good friend. I wish I could say I've always come through, but the truth is I haven't. There were times I didn't take people's broken hearts very seriously. Times when I was too damn tired to care. It can be hard to be kind when you're frustrated. Mostly I was able to be there for my pals when they needed me, but in the instances where I know I let someone down, I still bristle at the memory.

It's through those hard lessons that I've learned to be a better friend to others. I look for opportunities to support the people I care about. I like being asked to help. When my friend Sam got in a car accident, I was happy to rush to the hospital and be tasked with holding a jar for him to pee in while he waited to be seen. Of course, the nurse came in and took off his neck brace about two minutes after he'd relieved himself in the container I still had in my hands, but, hey, that's what friends are for.

I also try to receive my circle of friends "as is," and sometimes they're kind of messed up. I have one dear old companion who is a kleptomaniac, not above stealing small things from my house, and another who delights in telling far-fetched stories that could not possibly be true. Both make me laugh. I'd rather give up the odd pair of sunglasses and indulge a few whims, than lose either of them as friends.

Whatever happens in the future, I hope that my friends past and present know they were loved when they were loved, and that if we're not still in touch because of them or because of me, it's OK. We were friends. It was real. And that's a good thing.

SONG FOR DAUGHTERS

This is a song for our daughters, 'cause there's something that they need to hear
We never know when it's our time to go, so let me be perfectly clear
You're gonna win, you're gonna lose
You're gonna walk yourself 'round in your shoes
'Till maybe one day it's you who will say

Don't be too hard on yourselves
You don't have to be somebody else
On the days when you most want to give up the ghost
Don't be too hard, don't be too hard on yourselves

Girl everyone wants to be beautiful, everyone looks in the mirror
And sees things they would change, feels some sort of pain
But I see your beauty so clear
It's in the way that you light up when you are doing the things that you love
Just how you are, that's the best part

So don't be too hard on yourselves
You don't have to be somebody else
On the days when you most want to give up the ghost
Don't be too hard, don't be too hard on yourselves

If Venus should smile down upon you, and you're lucky enough to find love
Give it all that you've got, 'cause good love takes a lot
Pray that that love is enough
And if it's not, how it can hurt, it's so much less than you deserve
If you're there one day, you'll hear me say

Don't be too hard on yourselves
You don't have to be somebody else
On the days when you most want to give up the ghost
Don't be too hard, don't be too hard on yourselves
This is a song for my daughters
Don't be too hard, don't be too hard on yourselves

CHAPTER 3
KIDS

BLISSFUL CHAOS

Emerson's famous quip that nothing great was ever achieved without enthusiasm crossed my mind as I endeavored to potty train yet another child. I was burnt out in the extreme on cleaning up poop and could not for the life of me understand how it had come to pass that wiping a small human's butt was part of my daily routine. It's not that I didn't know how these things happened, it's that it kept happening. Somehow, we went from two, maybe three, to four small children and a cat that had to take Prozac in order to survive our household. Our days had filled with a chaos that was, at times, blissful but also in such constant flux that it was impossible to catch our breath.

I mean, I had read and enjoyed Ayn Rand. I was prepared to remain selfish forever, and what's more, I felt good about the decision. The world was overpopulated, and my own experiences with boyhood were less than stellar—it felt like an inconvenient layover on the way to becoming an adult. I know that will probably make my parents sad to read, but Mom, Dad...it was me not you. Seriously.

Raising kids, if I did it at all, was going to be something done on my terms, and if executed correctly, the outcome would be good, the obligations would be met, and the box would be checked. That was the entirety of the plan. Instead, here I was covered in shit and explaining to my other kids why the tooth fairy was a total bonehead for failing to show up last night.

My wife had been away less than 24 hours, and the situation was already growing dire. She is to our household as Mickey Mouse is to Disney. Without her the brand is completely thrown off. I didn't want to admit it, of course, because Kirsten had been skeptical when I first said I would be available to stay with the children for the long weekend. She was thinking of visiting some friends from college out west, and I told her I thought it was a great idea.

"Who would watch the kids?" she wondered aloud.

"Uh, hello? Me. I'm their dad. It's not babysitting if you're their dad."

She seemed unsure, but she needed the break, and we figured, what could go wrong? I had looked after them by myself loads of times before, so why should this go-round be any different? Somewhere between the tooth fairy inquisition and me yelling at the top of my lungs that I was not anybody's servant, I started to feel abysmal about my parenting skills and tried to remember why we had kids in the first place.

KIDS ARE THE WORST

You don't have to be a parent to know that kids are the worst. They break everything and almost never show any remorse for having done so. They are messy and get their fingerprints all over the walls and furniture. They forget to wash their hands and are always coming down with the flu on the first day of vacation. They do not hesitate to point out your bald spot, and as teenagers they can decimate you with their open hostility. Your mere existence can be an affront to them. You are in the way of their doing whatever they want, whenever they want, and with whomever they choose. I took my kids to see Ed Sheeran in concert, and on the way there we got into a squabble. I was making my case and asserted that I was a pretty cool dad. They told me they thought I was overplaying my hand.

My Sophia is 14 now. She has a boyfriend, feelings that I'm not always privy to, and a social agenda that, like any respectable teen, she keeps at a safe distance from her parents. We worry. Not because of anything in particular—she's doing great—but because how can we not? She's our baby. The problem is, she's not actually a baby anymore.

One night I heard Kirsten ask her a question three times in a row with no response. I walked into the kitchen to find Soph staring at her phone, and I told her to put it down immediately and answer her mother. When she didn't, I grabbed for it and suddenly found my daughter screaming at me not to touch her.

It gutted me. The force of the unexpected reaction and the sting of the words. She was my first born, and I was the second person to ever hold her on this earth, but now the mere grazing of my hand across her own was an unwelcome slight. She seemed so upset, and neither Ki nor I had any real idea why. Maybe she didn't either. That's the thing about adolescence; it's a hard sea to navigate for both the adolescent and the adult.

And then there are the hormones—the chemicals creating a slew of unfamiliar feelings for the kid, which in turn keep the curve balls coming at the parents (who at this point have a tendency to become increasingly irrational themselves). It's no surprise, then, that most teenagers start to feel their peers are far more important than their parents. You hardly know what do to with yourself at that age, but you just *know* that your folks don't have the answer.

As parents we have expectations that we hope our children will meet, some of which are fair and some of which are most certainly not, but damn if I can tell the difference. It can be hard to distinguish between simple vexation (*Why don't they appreciate Van Morrison more?*) and justifiable disappointment (*How can they have lied to me?*). Meanwhile our kids go from thinking we are the greatest to, in the blink of an eye, finding fault with everything we do. Parents: the great embarrassment.

I told Sophia that words have power, sometimes more than we realize, and that I was really hurt by her response. It made me feel uncomfortable. But then again, it did get my attention, and is it really her job to make me comfortable? Who am I kidding? There is no bigger drama queen in our household than me, and I say something I don't mean at least once a week, probably more. We all do.

I felt like I should be teaching her a lesson, but what I really wanted was to give her a hug and ease whatever she was feeling. Exposed, shaken, and still a little pissed off, I didn't know what to do. One look at my wife revealed that she clearly didn't either. It's all well and good to say that children need boundaries. Make a rule, stick to the rule. Nice. Neat. But what do you do when the guidelines you established don't cover the ever-shifting territory you find yourself in? Were we supposed to be disciplining this behavior or giving her space? Could we have somehow anticipated a when-dad-grabs-the-phone-because-you're-not-paying-attention-you're-not-to-curl-up-on-the-floor-and-yell-back-at-him scenario? There are things you can't see coming until they are right in front of you.

Ki and I spend most of our nights in unofficial war room strategy sessions, trying to navigate the various challenges, emotions, and requests of our four kids. For the most part, we're glad to do it and to have each other to validate our thinking. I know both of us find our role as parents to be one of the more fulfilling aspects of midlife, but sometimes it's pretty freaking stressful. All the careful planning and books in the world won't prep you for how you're going to feel when your kid fights back or, worse, makes a really sensible point that forces you to reconsider your long-held belief. It's *intense.*

Kirsten once said that when Sophia and I disagree, it's like watching me debate with myself. I don't think she meant it as an insult, just an observation. And in moments of great passion, which this was, sometimes an unemotional take on things is exactly what's called for. I found myself thinking about what usually drove me the craziest in an argument: a lack of compassion, a feeling that I wasn't being heard. I started there.

Cooler heads prevailed, we recalibrated, and my daughter and I got our equilibrium back. I tucked Sophia in that night and retreated to my bedroom so I could privately obsess over the way I had handled every aspect of the night's drama. I have a feeling she did the exact same thing.

KIDS ARE THE BEST

I became a parent on January 7, 2005. I woke up to find my partner in crime Swiffering the house. She cleaned with determination and purpose. "It's time."

"Why are you mopping the floor then?" I asked, wiping the sleep from my eyes.

"Because it's time."

Ten hours later, one of the four greatest things I would

ever do with my life introduced herself to me by way of an arresting look from magnificent walnut-brown eyes. That night she stared back at me through the dim light that leaked in from outside the door of our hospital room, and I knew love. And what is our life if not a measure of the amount of love we give and receive?

After Sophia was born, a bit of my previous idiocy washed away. I no longer bothered to consider the option of not liking kids. The affection my wife and I now had for our child was a one-way street. The little girl would care about us, too, no doubt, but not in the same way we would her. It was a wonderful sensation, though from time to time we'd look at each other apologetically, clear in the knowledge that there was a new occupant holding the number one seed in each of our hearts.

In spite of my original plan to follow Tom Petty's example and keep the details of my personal life private, within 24 hours I had written a song for my new baby that revealed pretty much everything but her Social Security number. I didn't know it then, but I was destined to become "Raffi for adults," singing about family every chance I got and powerless to resist the pull of the motif. I was forever changed.

In the days that followed, an analogy took shape in my mind. It was of a mansion on the hill. I imagined what it would be like to drive by the house of your dreams every day and see it in all its splendid glory. Flawlessly appointed, with plenty of open space and beautiful landscaping; the inside would be idyllic, too, with each amenity custom-tailored to your liking, though you'd only know this from pictures. In my fantasy, one day a stranger hands over a set of keys. When you ask what's going on, you learn that the house is yours. Free and clear. No mortgage to pay. You walk inside and it's just as you had imagined, extraordinary and yours to live in forever. That's what loving a child is like.

● ⋯⋯⋯⋯⋯⋯⋯ ● ⋯⋯⋯⋯⋯⋯ ●

From infants to teenagers, being a kid is all about firsts. First smile. First solid food. First steps. First teeth. First day of school. First best friend. First recital. First game. First sleepover. First Kiss. First Car. First place of your own… and off you go. Somewhere along the way, a lot of us adults stop having firsts. Why? Stuff used to be so exciting. A worm in the garden? Fantastic. A beautiful yellow dress in the window of a store? Let's go back and look at it again! A game of "spa" where we rub Mom's and Dad's feet? OK, I'll admit I never played that one, but I loved when my own kids went through a phase where they were into it.

The point is that when we're younger, we keep moving. We search. We seek. We adapt to our surroundings. It's incredible to watch and even more incredible to think back on actually having been that way. Children know how to rebound. There's something so beautiful about the fact that little kids don't always know to be sad when something sad has happened. On 9/11, babies went to sleep the same as they always had, unfettered by the course of events that had just altered history. It helps heal the rest of us by association. It keeps us from falling into our own despair.

My youngest was born a few months after my mother-in-law passed away. We all kind of hit the wall and were moving through our days in a fog, and then came little Greta, unaware of our grief and oblivious to anything other than the task of being a newborn. Because of her we learned to smile again more quickly than we otherwise might have.

If you want to see resilience up close, care for an infant. If you want to have more firsts, volunteer with toddlers and try seeing the world through their eyes for a while. If you want to be reminded that your problems are not the only problems, talk to a teenager. It won't be long before they'll have you convinced that no one's troubles since the dawn of man can match their own.

I swore I would never forget what it felt like to be 15 and

ostracized, but the second I got to college that's exactly what happened. I buried those feelings at the very first chance I got. I'm guessing it's like that for a lot of us. Kids remind us of certain things we've tried to erase from memory. They force us to own up to our past. Sometimes we can see our flaws reflected in our children, and often those are the very things that make us the most angry or impatient. That can be terrifying, and if we try to tell them about it, we will definitely be called weird. But now that I'm older, I know weird can be good.

KIDS ARE THE WORST

Kids also cost a lot of money, and you have to remind them for years to say "please" and "thank you" before they catch on. Some never do. When they're small, they smell like delicious blueberry muffins (the whole diaper situation notwithstanding), but by the time they are young adults, they're more like a walking gym locker that needs constant reminding to Febreze itself. They're also very noisy. They squeal, chitter, and honk their way around with almost no regard for how they're affecting others—like a group of businessmen in a bar, they aren't the best when it comes to using their "indoor voices."

I can remember before I had kids of my own, I noticed two things about people I knew who had recently become parents. The first was that they used to be more fun. The second was that it was awful to receive unsolicited endorsements for why everyone else needed to procreate.

"It's amazing—you guys are gonna love it. We aren't getting much sleep, of course, and haven't had sex in months, or even really gone on a date since the baby came... but you guys should totally have kids too!" A sucker is born every minute, I guess.

Infertility has been rising for decades, and many of us have made a conscious choice to not have children, but our college roommate and their spouse might be so blinded by their new arrival that they feel the need to convince every couple they meet to start reproducing. It's like telling a poor person that they ought to get some money and expecting them to thank you for it. I chalked it up to misery loves company.

Now that I am a father, I can't even feign impartiality on the topic because like the other crazies, I am enamored with my offspring. But I do remember how annoying it was to have parent-mania foisted upon me. This is not that. I'm not saying that your relationship with children is important because I think everyone needs to have them. I'm saying it because the way we treat children, with all their hope and vulnerability, is a direct tie-in to the kind of people that we are.

KIDS ARE THE BEST

Another thing I love about young people is that they haven't ceased to dream. They still believe. And if they're fledgling enough, kids will believe *anything.* I mean, hello, Santa Claus? Consider the mechanics of how a large man could fit in the chimney of every single house throughout the world in the course of one night without so much as a broken vase. You'd have to be a few sandwiches short of a picnic to buy that one, but most kids do. In our household I've avoided making any firm commitments when it comes to Kris Kringle. I dodge those questions like no other. I know that makes me sound like a humbug, but my logic is that if I lie to them about the Elf on the Shelf, maybe they won't listen to me when I tell them to stay away from crystal meth. *We couldn't trust that guy growing up, why should we believe him now?*

Kids learn a lot outside of the home too. Probably too much. When we're little, we have faith in almost everyone.

The older boy down the street who insists that smoking isn't a big deal, the friend of the family who takes it upon themselves to tell us we'll need to "get a real job" when we share our youthful aspirations with them, the bigoted relative who spreads their brand of casual racism by telling us off-color jokes. As a child you're taking all this in and processing it. I know I was. These aren't hypothetical examples. If your uncle, the alcoholic, is telling 7-year-old you that "you haven't lived until you've stuck your hand up a cow's ass," you'd better hope there are some alternate narratives being shared.

That's why teachers are so important. The ripples set in motion from a good or bad educator can extend for years and be the difference between a productive member of society and a disenfranchised criminal. If you think I'm being melodramatic, recall what kind of mentors you had that allowed you to make that distinction. I read the other day that the top 25 hedge fund managers make more than all the nation's kindergarten teachers combined. With due respect to my many friends in finance, that pisses me off. If it weren't for my teachers, I'd still believe that anti-Semitism was no longer an issue and that AIDS only affected gay men. I'd have no idea how to budget my finances, and I certainly wouldn't be able to write this book. Educators have a direct impact on the lives of millions and yet remain some of the most undercompensated workers in the country.

I speak and perform at different types of schools all the time, and even though I still get back-to-school jitters when I walk through those doors, I am always amazed to witness young people's capacity to learn. They have fabulous bull-shit detectors, and if you're going to interact with them, you'll have to be real or you're toast. They respect truth and despise a fake.

I love going to elementary schools the most. If you're lucky enough to get the little ones talking, they'll ask so many questions, you can almost see their belief systems taking shape in front of your very eyes. Last year I visited a group of first-graders at a school outside Chicago. When I finished my presentation, I opened up the floor to questions, "Does anyone want to ask me about anything we just talked about?"

A girl raised her hand, "I'm gonna have a little sister."

"Oh, that's wonderful," I answered.

Then a boy raised his hand, "I saw *The Good Dinosaur.*"

"Wow, those are really great questions," I said. Kids are the best.

KIDS ARE THE WORST

But sometimes, kids get sick. Sometimes they get really sick and we see just how powerless we are. That's a hard one. I've played at a lot of children's hospitals. I've met the parents, the caretakers, and the kids. They're always brave. I always walk away inspired, and there hasn't been one time when I was able to give them even a fraction of what they gave me, but still...pediatric cancer? It's so fucking unfair.

And it's not just catastrophic illnesses that we wish we could shield them from. Because of their physical size and dependence on adults, they are easy marks. We face any number of problems here. In addition to gangs, eating disorders, suicide, and depression, we've now also got addictions to opioids, pornography, and technology, not to mention an internet-driven human-trafficking crisis that does not appear to be going away anytime soon.

Even our schools don't feel safe the way they once did. How did we get to a place where the President of the United States vilifies students who fight for stronger gun laws after enduring a school shooting? I never in my wildest dreams thought I would see that day. Only in my worst nightmares could I have conceived that something like Sandy Hook was even possible. But it happened, seven miles from my home where my own first-grader was in lockdown that same day. If we don't stem the tide of these dark tendencies, we will have failed the next generation, and yet I'm afraid these are also the things that are the hardest to protect them from.

So we don't. Instead, we focus on the day-to-day events from which they should not need shielding. Rights of passage that are increasingly denied them by overprotective parents. A chance to get dumped. A chance to deal with a flat tire without a call to mom or dad. A chance to go out with friends without having to text home every hour. A chance to cook their own meals and clean their own clothes; to fill out their own college applications. A chance to climb a mountain or catch a wave or...*fail*.

We drive them here and there, partake in their social lives, sign them up for everything. We orchestrate play dates when they're little and do dinners with the parents of their love interests when they're teens. If we don't participate or can't afford to, we are racked with guilt and feel as though we're depriving them. It's hard for me to imagine how any of this helps them grow into functional adults. If we don't set them up for independence, how will they ever be independent?

I can feel myself overdoing it. Pretending that if they play by all the rules and listen to what I tell them, everything will work out perfectly. But it's a lie. Life is going to be hard, and the problems they will face will be large, so they'll need to be capable and resourceful.

Kids aren't the worst because they get sick or because they are taken advantage of. None of those conditions are their fault. Kids are the worst because once we start loving them, we can't go back, and that's like having your heart walk around outside your body.

BLISSFUL CHAOS REVISITED

When Kirsten arrived home from the airport, she looked beautiful and rested. I hadn't shaved or showered in four days and my nerves were pretty well shot. The axis of our home life had been reinstated, and despite it being touch-and-go for a while, I knew that it would all be just fine.

In her absence I had learned some things I didn't know about these little creatures I'd been sharing a residence with; like when Noelle asks for "orange juice" in actuality she wants milk mixed with prune juice; and a "tomato" is obviously a sweet potato. I discovered that you couldn't be cavalier and use the phrase "scaredy-cat" unless you were prepared to see Greta vigilantly combing the house in search of the scary cat. I found out that Adeline had been sleeping with my own boyhood teddy bear, Georgie, and that it wasn't all that long ago when I, too, was afraid of the dark.

On the last night of my solo voyage, I declared it was bedtime and was told I was "just like mom and the babysitters"; I took some comfort in that. Nevertheless, I was exhausted. Thankfully, there is nothing like a weekend away from your kids to remind you how much you enjoy them, and in Kirsten's face I could see the mansion on the hill. That was always enough for me. The children brought us there and kept us there. Together again, everything felt right, even if some of my parental tactics had seemed quite wrong.

I wasn't always this way. I made a choice to love kids. That changed me. I got hooked on the notion of atonement. The idea that we can be redeemed by making the lives of children better than the ones we ourselves are living out. Adults are in the position of power, and how we use it says nothing about the child and everything about us. Whatever I might have said, you and I both know...kids are the best.

ALL THE LOVE (THAT COMES TO ME)

We'll drink enough alcohol to raise these kids, warts and all
There wasn't enough alcohol to quench my parents' thirst
If I end up just like them, that's OK, ain't no sin
Where you're going, where you've been, it's mostly the same place

I've got all I ever wanted
But I still cannot believe
How I love to take for granted
All the love that comes to me

We've got enough words to write, books to read, fights to fight
There ain't enough thoughts and prayers to satiate my rage
Maybe we are just as bad as our worst enemies have said
Or maybe we are just ourselves and having an off day

I've got all I ever wanted
But I still cannot believe
How I love to take for granted
All the love that comes to me

I dig the evening buzz, I hate the morning drag, I dig the evening buzz
And I don't sleep nearly enough but I'm still happy because,
I am still happy because...

I've got all I ever wanted
All I'll ever need
And I love to take for granted
All the love that comes to me

You are all that I ever wanted
I still cannot believe
That I love to take for granted
All the love...that comes...to me

CHAPTER 4
PARENTS

Parents: Adults held up to superhuman standards that they inevitably fall short of, enduring both deserved and undeserved judgment from their children.

THE PAST

D inner was getting cold on the table as my parents argued in that strained way that people argue when they are furious with one another but trying to not raise their voices. A loud contorted whisper. I lay on the fuzzy wall-to-wall carpet beneath the table listening to their 11-year marriage unravel. It is my third-earliest memory. Prior to that, I remember that we drove to Virginia for a family camping trip, and I didn't wear a seatbelt because we didn't make a big deal about seatbelts then. Nowadays, car seat manufacturers send you a notice every other year that could be paraphrased, *Unless you hate your kids and want them to be injured, you'll buy our newest model immediately because what we recently sold you is dangerous.* But in 1980, automotive safety wasn't what it is today.

My other early memory is of cracking my forehead open at preschool. A ham even at age 3, I slid across the floor in an effort to impress a girl and met head on with a steel beam. I got 13 stitches and can still recall the fluorescent lights and gas mask as the doctor put me under at the hospital. I have a Harry Potter–like scar there to this day, commemorating where the healing took place. There ought to be a mark like that across my heart too.

Although it made me sad when my dad moved out, I was a kid and kids bounce back, so I adjusted and learned to accept our new reality. My parents decided to live close to one another for the sake of my sister, Amy, and I. That was a generous act on their part. We split our time between the two houses, and my dad married my stepmother, Carol, about five years later.

My folks had been teenagers when they got together, and I suppose marriage, like most anything else, takes time and practice. When both of them eventually did remarry, they seemed to get it more *right* the second time around. In terms of finding a suitable companion, sometimes we're old enough to start having sex but still too young to recognize where our life might be headed. There's no real way of knowing if our needs will be aligned with our partner's. If only they taught us that in high school chemistry instead of the periodic table. But in the end, it takes more than science to make us parents anyway; biology is only part of the equation.

Nurture versus nature. I had both. I can imagine that being a stepparent could be a tough gig, but mine made it look easy. They loved me, and I loved them. It was kind of that simple. I believe there is a lot more to being a good parent than loving your kids, but it begins there. In theory, even a total degenerate should be able to convey affection for their kin. How hard is it to say, "I'm a mess, but that doesn't mean I don't love you"? Or maybe "I think *you're* a mess, but that doesn't mean I don't love you"?

Unfortunately, emotional blockage is one of the many traditions passed on from generation to generation. Even really good people sometimes suck at letting their children know they are loved, and plenty of us, in order to feel better about our own shortcomings, have convinced ourselves that we were unloved. But by the time we're in our 30s, we really would do better to take responsibility for our life as it stands, regardless of what our parents did or did not do. When we keep blaming them, we give away our power as though we have no control over our future because of our past.

Me? I always knew I was loved. That helped. I learned from my mom how to clean a toilet and do laundry. She taught me cooking and all manner of household chores so that I'd "never have to depend on a woman" to do these things for me. We had crystals all around our home, and although it was considered new age at the time, she, more than anyone else, taught me to believe in a universal power higher than myself.

I was a latchkey kid, happily independent, and if she was molding me to be the kind of man she was missing in her own life, it was a subtext that I was happy to oblige. It's a lucky thing to have a parent who cares about your development as much as they do your comfort. I'm pretty sure ease is the gateway drug to entitlement, and entitlement is a dead end. But that could also be my New England Protestant upbringing at work.

When I almost walked out the door for a date my junior year of high school with no money in my pocket, my mother loaned me $50 and told me I would need to reimburse her. I paid her back the money, but I can never repay the debt for having helped me get off on the right foot with my future wife.

My dad read me books and played me classic rock records. I was a crap athlete, but nonetheless he would pitch me balls for hours, take me skiing, enroll me in camps, and replace the basketball hoop in our driveway every single time the local kids stole it—the neighborhood was not what you would call dangerous, but not entirely safe either. We lived in a duplex where I once found a live rat in the toilet, and I had multiple bikes hijacked right out from underneath me. Whatever drama may have been playing out, he was easygoing and never raised his voice at my siblings or me. When I consider how much I've yelled at my own children, I find that almost inconceivable, but I've seen it up close and because of him, I know it can be done.

I wasn't a bad kid, but I definitely wasn't a choirboy either. I drank my share of alcohol and snuck out kind of a lot. Kirsten lived about 45 minutes away, and once we started dating, the stealthy behavior hit another gear. I would tell my mom I was sleeping at my dad's, my dad I was sleeping at my mom's, and I'd drive my beat-up orange Hyundai Excel covered in Grateful Dead stickers to the cul-de-sac where she lived. I'd knock on her window and we'd hang out listening to music, talking, and kissing until the wee hours of the morning.

All those years of covert operations, including a few Ferris Bueller–style morning exits, and we never got caught. I figured some great cosmic power wanted us to be together. The irony, of course, is that now I have four daughters of my own, all of whom are likely to read this book and hold it over my head. But that's their job, that's what we do to our parents. We evaluate them and use their lives as a tool to shape our own. I might raise my voice more than my father and never be as fully domesticated as my mother may have wished, but I knew, even then, that when I grew up, I would marry once, and I would love her for the rest of my life if it killed me.

●················●··············●

These are my memories of being a kid. With the addition of my in-laws, I was brought into adulthood by six smart, loving, and attentive parents. One hundred and fifty-three million orphans on the planet in need of someone to look out for them, and I got six guardians. It hardly seems fair.

What I remember is solidified in my own mind as fact, but the truth is, it's hard to trust a memory. My kids have been to Italy, Disney, and any number of other places they claim to have no recollection of having gone. Sometimes they'll say, "Dad, I wonder if you can be at my birthday party this year?" Mind you, I have never, not even once, missed one of my children's birthday parties. I'm not saying we haven't moved a few around to accommodate a schedule here and there, but I've never missed one. I care. I'm trying.

Children, however, are under no mandate to remember it that way, and *that*, while not easy to concede, is *their* right. Accepting that our kids are beyond our control, that their life is theirs to live, and that our contribution to molding them in youth does not allow us to lay claim to their adulthood is not always easy, to say the least. All you can really do as a parent is share the best information you have—you know, lead the horse to water and all that. You can offer up your bits of hardscrabble experience and moments of clarity, and if you manage to do so with a kindness of spirit, well that's a double win. The pearls of wisdom may not always sink in, but it's still important that they get extended.

Also, as children we need to know that our parents care for us more than themselves. To expect more than that of any parent is to ask an awful lot, though that will never stop us from expecting it.

THE PRESENT

I don't smoke pot.

Last fall, though, my stepfather, "Pa," was very ill. He was a straight edge Italian guy who hadn't smoked anything or drunk alcohol in decades. He had done the 12-step program long before I met him, so I never knew his wild side. It takes courage to deal directly with one's demons, and he had done so. I respected him.

Maybe because he wasn't my biological father, I tended to be more open to his quirky life lessons, but for whatever reason I allowed him to teach me with very little resistance. How to plant grass, build a stone wall, lay asphalt, cut down a tree, get rid of ants, split wood, set up a mouse trap, buy a car, paint a fence, sell a product, commit to a relationship, and so on and so forth.

His two sons by birth, my stepbrothers, are both handy guys. Despite his tutelage, I still am not. I often felt like Steve Martin in the opening scene of *The Jerk,* where he tells his African-American family that he "doesn't know what it is, but he feels like he's different." I'd think of that movie whenever I had to call Pa to help me undo some minor homespun disaster I had created. He would refer to me as his son and act as though whatever I had done was "not too bad at all," even though he usually had to take my work apart and start again from scratch.

Kirsten might see me with a hammer and nail, and with an alarmed look on her face ask where I was going.

"I can hang a picture in my own house."

"Are you sure you don't want to call someone?"

"Yes, I'm sure."

An hour later, once I had made a mess of whatever it was I happened to be working on, I would call Pa.

●·················●·················●

As I mentioned, though, he was sick now, suffering from stage IV pancreatic cancer and beginning to lose the fight. His doctor recommended medicinal marijuana. Initially he resisted, but after a time he agreed to try it, only to find the dispensary drugs too strong for his liking. It occurred to me that I worked in a profession where, to state it delicately, the use of marijuana is quite popular. "I've got friends who can help," I told Pa, taking some pride in my role as middleman. And so, for a season I suppose you could say I was working as a dealer, getting Pa the sativa oil that seemed to be just right for his pain management.

When he passed away, I went to see my friend, the supplier, and he invited me to smoke with him.

"I'm good, thank you," I declined, figuring that would be the end of it.

"C'mon, man, for your dad."

Well, damn, if you put it like that...

So we headed out to the garage, and the first red flag should have been that he pulled out a bong. Having not seen one of those up close since college, I might have known I was out of my depth, but lest we parents forget, "Just saying no" is easier said than done. There we were, two fortysome-things, sitting on folding chairs behind the cars in case our kids happened to walk in and catch us smoking grass. You spend half your teenage years hiding from your parents and then become an adult only to end up hiding from your kids.

So my pal does his thing, burning through a few bowls, while I'm one hit deep and coughing out the words "all set." I'm a little light-headed, but everything is basically fine as we make small talk and...get high. We're about to go back inside when he says to me, "Stephen, I want you to try this stuff. It's called shatter. It's really smooth, and I think you're going to love it." Red flag number two!

Although I am constantly telling my kids not to give in to peer pressure, before I can even process the request, I hear myself say, "OK, sure, if you think I'll like it." No resistance at all. Another thing about being a parent: Do as I say, not as I do.

From a silk pouch comes an additional glass contraption that looks even more sinister, like what they use to smoke crack in. He takes a tiny blowtorch out and is heating it up. Isn't this what they do to heroin? I'm about to do the sensible thing and leave when he passes me the...um...pipe, at which point I put my lips on it and suck in. I take one hit—not even—and with stunning immediacy, I feel like a Smurf. Jokey Smurf specifically. *Beep-beep-beep-beep-beep.* My hands are big, white, soft, furry mitts.

We skulk back inside where we encounter one of his children. I see an otherwise adorable 4-year-old looking up at me, and all I can think is, *She knows everything.* On cue my phone rings, and it's my newly widowed mother. She's crying and wants to know if I can come over. Because I'm ill-equipped to do anything more than try not to swallow my own tongue, I am forced to decline her invitation and inform her that I am too stoned to drive. Guy knows how to make his mother proud, eh?

My buddy is sitting on the couch looking like the Cheshire Cat, and I make him promise me I'm not on crack. When we get home later, Kirsten says to me, "I've never heard you say that little for that long." I don't respond because I'm still baked, but that doesn't change the fact that I'm also still a dad. The kind of dad who craves absolutes but figures out everything as he goes. The guy's guy whose daughters hold him up as the example of what a man is supposed to be, even as he waits in fear for the day when they realize just how imperfect he is.

• • • • • • • • • • • • • • • •

Finding the whole experience of Pa's passing overwhelming, I book a boys' trip to Dallas with my father, father-in-law, and my two brothers-in-law. I make all the arrangements, but that doesn't keep Steve Kellogg, Sr. from telling me what to do everywhere we go. "Don't park there, the car will get hot in the sun." "Here's what you do, Stephen, you go to the check-in and get a couple extra bags of peanuts in case you get hungry later." "Tell our server what you want to drink when they seat us so that we can place our dinner order when the waiter returns."

He's pulled himself away from his men's group, the Romeos (which stands for Retired Old Men Eating Out), and I think he's got some excess energy to burn by hovering over me with instructions. We're taking a leak at the airport when my dad, too loudly, begins a short lecture on sanitary habits: "Grab a paper towel and use it to open the handle of the bathroom stall."

I find myself daydreaming about whether I might know more than he does at this point, but my train of thought gets broken when he asks me to "run and grab some ice from the ice machine because there is nothing better than filling the sink with ice and putting your beers in there."

We share a hotel room and can't agree on the temperature. It feels like a Jamaican rain forest to me and yet he's shivering under the covers, asking for a few more degrees on the thermostat. His oversized and well-worn tighty-whities billowing behind him as he jumps up to get more layers, I notice he looks a little older than the last time I saw him. "How long have you had that underwear?" I ask.

"These? I don't know."

"Might be time for some new ones, Pop. Those are looking a little broken in."

"There are no holes," he protests.

"Dad, you can get a 10-pack at Marshalls for like $20. You might feel a little...cleaner in them. I'll get you some for Christmas." The timbre of my voice is the same one I use with my second-grader. It makes my heart skip a beat, and I relent on the climate of the room. Falling asleep that night I reprimand myself for having been irritated earlier. He would take a bullet for me. Does anything else really matter?

THE FUTURE

Both of my parents are in the process of moving into smaller houses now. Their parents have died, and their children have left the home. Like birds, they migrate into humbler stations. It's sad to say goodbye to the better memories of those dwellings I grew up in, but I'm so busy, I manage to do so in about an hour, and then slip back into my own routine. I remind myself what a relief it is to have them settled in less overwhelming situations. They seem relieved too. Also, though, scared.

We all know what's ahead. Not the details, but the outcome is certain. We thought we understood the agreement: Parents are supposed to teach kids, right? They're the parent, I'm the kid; they teach me. Well, then, why am I on the phone explaining how to use the computer? Why doesn't my dad know when it's time to upgrade underwear? Why do they need me so much? Why do I still need them so much?

● • • • • • • • • • • • • • • • • • ● • • • • • • • • • • • • • • • ●

I went to see Pa about a month before he passed away. I asked him what I could be doing better. He was tired. He had written three books in his last two years, continued to maintain the house and his health, traveled with Mom, and attended the Little League games of his grandkids, all while feeling pretty sick. He sighed, "Stephano, just keep doing what you're doing." I was looking for more. He handed me a book from the 1980s called *Creating Midlife*. After he was gone, I soldiered through what felt like banal advice when toward the back I found a Post-It note. "Start with this book. I will be working on the items you requested. This will help you on your journey. Love, Pa."

Not a dry eye in the house.

Not long ago I was afraid I had a brain tumor and didn't sleep for three days as I tossed, turned, and waited for an appointment to assess the growth on my head. The evening before the doctor was to see me, I saw my dad who felt the bump and said nonchalantly, "A wen."

I beg your pardon? "Oh, yeah, that's a sebaceous cyst. I get them all the time."

"Well, hell, Dad, can you make me a checklist of other things I should be on the lookout for?"

"Just a wen," he repeated. No list.

No parent will ever know precisely how well he or she did in their role. Kids will say their mom and dad messed them up, and the hard reality is, that may be true. Good parents raise bad kids. Bad parents raise good kids. The same parents can raise two children who turn out to be entirely different from one another. Our kids may be a reflection of us, but they will never be a mirror image. For all the books I've read on how to raise children, I can only deduce that we think we know, but we don't really know.

What I am certain of is this: I was loved, and therefore I believe I was parented. It's all we can rightfully expect. I send postcards home to my kids when I'm on tour in the hopes that someday, when they're in therapy, they'll at least know I was making an effort.

I now find myself in the head role, criticized and revered at the same time. In charge for a moment, aware that someday not far from this very day, perhaps, I'll be the one shuffling around in old undies unable to reach my kids because they're off smoking pot with their friends.

●·················●·················●

Parents: Adults who love their children more than themselves and do the best they can regardless of outcome.

ORION

Orion, I can see you looking down
Small houses that we built into the ground
At a distance you can't see what's falling down
If you're up close you can almost hear the sound

Of summer, I remember
We would pack our things into the car, although we never got too far
It's a wonder to discover how the winter finds its way to spring
Being young meant everything in the summer

Constellations, are you laughing at us all?
We rage, as we watch our heroes fall
If they're up there, remember them to me
Like my grandpa on the beach of Normandy

In the summer, we remember
While Orion's sword is burning out
Lovers long forgotten now, there were mothers
Who discovered how the winter finds its way to spring
Your parents don't know everything in the summer

Oh, the stars are still the same
Oh, they see all of our pain
Oh, they can't do anything
And slowly they explode

Orion, to be young and insecure
It's the trade-off, it's the cost of wanting more

Every summer, remember
To pack your things into the car and if you never get too far
Take a number, discover
You'll be doing what your parents did, don't you dare forget it kid
In the summer, I remember
That Orion's sword is burning out, all will be forgotten now in the summer

CHAPTER 5

HEROES

One day this battle will be over. The struggle will conclude, and we will no longer need to prove our worth or suffer feelings of inadequacy. Until then, we strive.

This is why we need heroes.

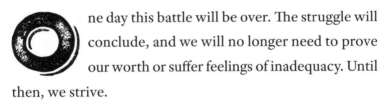

My daughters are staring at a screen again. Scrolling. Studying the lives of others. As Theodore Roosevelt said, "Comparison is the thief of joy."

Something about it feels wrong to me, and that turns me a little preachy. It gets me thinking about people I don't like; the ones we look up to for the wrong reasons. Then I start in.

"You know, just because the cool kids don't accept you, that doesn't mean you aren't a cool kid. It's easy to be fooled into thinking that other people's lives are tidy and neat, when in fact they are messy just like ours." I end up way off topic. I say all this to them, but they must know I'm talking to myself.

I reference Lincoln, Dickens, Taylor Swift, and my grandfather in a matter of minutes, and although my girls are confused as to how they ended up on the receiving end of a lecture about whom we idolize and lavish our attention upon, I think I've actually hit a nerve.

Life can be an absolute shit-show, unraveling in front of our very eyes, and yet the knowledge that people went before us and somehow not only got through it but also made something special happen—that's amazing. Mentors, idols, role models, and those who, in the face of adversity, acted the way we dream we could; these are what I'm calling heroes. It's nice to imagine an elevated version of humanity, and it's easier to believe in when we can pay witness to the inspiring behavior of our fellow human beings. Through their aspiration, we are taught to shoot for the stars. These people show us who we want to be.

Again, this is why we need heroes.

WHAT ARE THE QUALITIES OF A HERO?

A small word with big implications. *Someone who is admired or idealized for outstanding achievements, courage, or noble qualities.* That's a succinct characterization, but it does leave a few flies in the ointment. We live in a time when we have more access to information than ever before, and thus we end up finding out that Bill Cosby is not who we thought he was, the presidents are not who we thought they were (in myriad ways), Lance Armstrong is on steroids, and Martha Stewart is going to jail for insider trading. It's easy to develop cynicism when you've spent a lifetime believing in someone's accomplishments only to learn that they're not as "noble" as you thought.

We used to celebrate Christopher Columbus's "discovery" of America every year with a little song about 1492 and a day off from school. Now we find out that he was enslaving Native Americans and spreading smallpox, clearing the way for a European land grab. What a letdown. At which point we stop applauding the backstory of such ill-gotten gains we may also start remembering him as a villainous conqueror, instead of solely as the bold adventurer they sold us as children. Columbus is a perfect example of someone who checked two of the boxes—courage and outstanding achievements—while appearing to have fallen well short in the noble qualities department. Does that make him less of a hero? Possibly. Either way, no one's tripping over themselves to make amends for how the West was won.

So if a reputation can't withstand scrutiny in the age of the information superhighway, where does that leave us? Who is left? It's either those we don't know a lot about or those we decide to accept as the fallible individuals that they are. And let's face it, the more we get to know people, the less we may like them. That doesn't change who they always were. But familiarity breeds contempt.

Everybody is a part of the freak show. The key is to find people we can look up to whose skeletons aren't so ghastly that we have to turn away.

●●●●●●●●●●●●●●●●●●●●●●●●●●●●●●●●●

I'm going to share three short stories about heroes. The first one is an exemplar to many, though not necessarily me.

The other two involve my own personal heroes. As for the one about John Daly...well let's just say it's an anecdote that happens to involve a memorable weekend of golf and some salty jokes. Reader be warned: I am about to recount dialogue that uses a few choice words and phrases. As I tell my kids, "If you decide to swear out in the world, that's your decision. I don't condone it, and I won't defend it, *but* I have found these words extremely useful in my own life."

Let's start with the dirty one. Great men sometimes have great flaws.

OUTSTANDING ACHIEVEMENTS

Most of us can appreciate a good underdog story. Only the Grinch wouldn't feel something watching a movie like *Rudy*. But for me it goes beyond that. I tend to get my inspiration from people who not only achieve outstanding things but do so from a vantage point of being remarkably average in all other respects. If Taylor Swift (yes, she's one of my heroes) is going to be that good at singing, dancing, and writing, I appreciate that her social life often seems to be a bit of a train wreck. If Dickens is going to pen the best novel ever written, the least he could do is work in a factory at the age of 12 and have a bazillion kids whom he raises with mixed results. Lord, I don't know what I'd do if Tom Petty hadn't had to overcome domestic abuse and drugs. If it sounds like I'm being small, you won't catch me disagreeing.

I adore the everyman because I am the everyman. I mean, seriously, I've managed to become a professional singer with a one-octave range. It's not that I can't enjoy your Whitney Houstons or Otis Reddings or Mozarts. It's just that I don't find them as magical as, say, Willie Nelson.

People like me tend to gravitate toward those we can identify with, and while I don't dispute that this inclination is 100 percent fueled by insecurity, I've noticed that I dig the things that remind me of...*me*. If we can see a part of ourselves in another who is doing what we dream of doing, it's easier to feel some ownership over their accomplishments.

And, certainly, outstanding achievements extend beyond athletics and the arts. Jonas Salk cured polio. Bill Gates founded Microsoft. And apparently someone named Raffaele Esposito is credited with having invented pizza, which, if it's true, will make him only the second inventor whose name I know by heart (the other being Eli Whitney, who invented the cotton gin—a fact that for some strange reason remains emblazoned in my memory).

What about those scientists who decided to get married

and have babies to see if they could make their children the best chess players on the planet? Their daughters ended up number one, two, and six. It's impressive, but there is no way I can get behind that. I just can't relate. And the way we relate, or fail to, with those we idolize, admire, or find heroic is exactly what makes them inspirational to us. Thus, when choosing heroes, we are seeking exaltation from someone whom it feels like we know personally.

Although we dance around the fire when a hero falls from grace because, for a moment, we were pretending they were perfect, it's always a relief to us petty mortals to hear that they are not. This is just who people are...even heroes. And of all my imperfect friends who have achieved outstanding things, few have triumphed more than legendary golfer John Daly.

John is one of golf's largest personalities and biggest proponents of the game. There is a whole subset of golfers who took up the sport and embraced it because of his example. He took it out of the country clubs and put it back in the people's hands. He's won two of the four majors and was the longest hitting driver the game had ever seen for nearly a decade.

In 2013, he reached out to me and asked to use some of my music for a beverage company he was starting. I agreed.

We struck up a friendship and, although there is plenty we disagree on, have remained friends ever since. I'm not much of a golfer, favoring a six iron from the tee box, but my father and fairly conservative father-in-law, whom you'll remember I'd been working to impress since high school, both are. So when John invited us to his hometown golf course in Dardanelle, Arkansas, we jumped at the chance.

I almost can't remember ever seeing my father-in-law so excited. Years earlier he had met someone who knew John, and stories about "Wild Thing" (one of John's nicknames) had a way of growing over time. He had played a course with someone who had played a course. Eagled a par five or some such business. Stuff that golfers get excited about. He mentioned it to me on the way there, and I reminded our entourage that my friend John was a lot of fun but also a little bit of a colorful character. *Just a heads up, guys.*

We arrived in town and met John at a local restaurant. He was on the back patio with his brother, daughter, and some friends when we got there. I gave him a hug and made the introductions. My wife's dad jumped right in, "I know someone who knows you."

John grinned. "Did I fuck her?"

I nearly choked on my teeth, but my father-in-law was evidently unfazed: "No, it's a he."

"Well, did he suck my cock?" Daly said without missing a beat.

"I'm gonna grab an iced tea and let you two catch up." I hightailed it to the back bar.

Before you get outraged (and I know some of you will), understand that this was John Daly being John Daly. The same guy who gave $30,000 to the widow of a fan killed in a lightning strike, long before he was a wealthy professional athlete. The dude who calls me every now and then just to tell me he loves me. He cares about his community and wants the best for his family—just like the rest of us. Unlike the rest of us, he happens to drive the ball 300 yards and ignore all kinds of social norms. It's the fact that he's relatable, though, that people love about JD. That's what I love about him anyway. He is unapologetically himself. And this is the paradox of heroism: If you've achieved something great, people might be jealous and scrutinize you, but they're just as likely to overlook your flaws through their rose-colored glasses.

COURAGE

"Never believe your own propaganda," my grandfather used to tell us.

His point is well taken. You're not as great (or as bad) as they'll say you are, so keep your own compass and steady on. Be graceful when you're winning and bold when the chips are down. If you rise in this life, turn around and extend a hand to help up those still climbing.

When I consider profiles in courage, it's no surprise, then, that my first thought is not of Harriet Tubman or Anne Frank or Martin Luther King Jr. or Victoria Leigh Soto (though they'd all make excellent candidates). Instead, when I think about what fortitude looks like up close, my thoughts go to a scared 8-year-old boy from Berlin. I know he was scared because he told me so, and somehow that feels easier to hang on to.

In the 1930s my grandfather's family escaped from the Nazis by the skin of their teeth. His father was a lawyer imprisoned by the newly formed Third Reich for having defended those falsely accused of the infamous Reichstag fire. He was an attorney to the communist leader Ernst Thaelmann, even though he didn't share the same political beliefs. (You have to remember the communists were the last party with any real shot at opposing Hitler's rise to power.) Upon his temporary release from the Gestapo, he gathered his wife and three boys, and in the middle of the night they traveled by train to England. Later they made their way to Madison, Wisconsin, and upon arriving in the states as a burgeoning teen, Jurgen Roetter, my future grandfather and youngest son of Friedrich Roedelheimer, became "Jack" and began a full-hearted assimilation into American society.

As was the custom of "the greatest generation," he enlisted after Pearl Harbor and, at 19, found himself approaching the coast of German-occupied France in an LCVP. It was June 8, 1944, D-Day plus 2. Although he spoke very little about the war, he had a soft spot for his grand-children and once told me that had he arrived on D-Day, he would not have survived. I can still remember how hard it hit me when I saw *Saving Private Ryan* and was finally able to visualize what it must have been like to "jump out into the water while still taking fire." Prior to watching that movie, it seemed like someone else's story. But it wasn't. He weighed 119 pounds, even less than me at that age, and there he was fighting his way onto the beach. I guess sometimes valor is nothing more than a refusal to retreat.

He was stationed in a regiment with Ernest Hemingway

and J.D. Salinger and had opinions about both men that were based on personal experience. When the war was over, he came back and married my grandmother who had been his best friend in high school. They never came out and said it outright, but I'm pretty sure they waited until they were married to consummate the relationship, which would also explain the speed with which they got hitched after his return. He earned a PhD in history, taught at the University of Wisconsin for a couple years, then worked for the CIA for a hot minute before deciding to become a stockbroker. When I was that age, I could barely get up the guts to ask for directions if I was lost, but here was gallant young Jack Roetter, boyhood refugee turned poster boy for the American dream.

Growing up I would spend a couple weeks each summer visiting my grandparents. In that time, we'd take long bike rides around western Massachusetts, play Parcheesi, and go to the movies. One summer he took me to the music store and bought me my first real guitar. He told me that if he could have been anything, he would have most liked to have been an orchestral conductor or a philosopher—it's never lost on me that two generations later, I get to be both.

On another visit he taught me how to shave. It's easy to take for granted, or lose track of, where you get a simple life skill like that, but now every time I shave, I think of him.

Once a year we'd go to the Metropolitan Opera in New York City and to the Marlboro Chamber Music Festival in Vermont. Back then I found the programming a little boring, but I never tired of the time spent talking to him. It was his outlook that I was drawn to. When things went wrong, as they inevitably did, he would joke that "you can't win, and you may lose."

At 17 I started college at the University of Massachusetts, and my dorm was less than a mile away from his house. I can still remember him turning me on to Dostoevsky, Epictetus, and champagne cocktails all in one night. Smart, but never pretentious, he knew how to function in all kinds of society. Never forgot where he came from. He got up and did what he had to do every day despite *eis im Arsch* (a German saying that translates literally to "ice in ass" and refers to a feeling of anxiety or nervousness). I wanted to be just like him.

One day when I was close to graduating, I went to visit him at his office. One of the guys that worked with him shared with me an account that I've never forgotten. Apparently a loud and menacing street gang had been loitering outside their building and was blasting music to the point of distraction. Instead of calling the police, he walked out and greeted the offending party. As the legend has it, he offered his own enthusiasm for classical music and then asked that they take their gathering elsewhere so that working folks could do just that. The gang apparently did exactly as he requested. If that's not how the story goes, it sounds just like him, and I'm inclined to think they recognized the majesty of his character.

He only lived for a couple weeks after being diagnosed with stomach cancer in the spring of 2003. Most of his coworkers never even knew he was sick until he passed away. He labored right up to the very end, until his body was entirely used up. As he lay in the hospital dying, he said, "The entrance is easier than the exit." It was another brilliant reflection in a life of great witticisms. He was frightened though. Of course he was. Who wouldn't be? But being brave has never been about not being afraid.

The last time we ever spoke I was calling him from the road. He hadn't talked to anyone in almost a day, so they put the phone up to his ear, and I told him that I loved him. He surprised us all when he said, "I love you, too, ol' boy" because "I love you" was never his style. It took a lot for him to put himself out there in that way, but courage comes in all kinds of forms. He never stopped learning.

James Allen said, "Circumstances do not make the man, they reveal him." Jack Roetter was revealed to me every time I saw him. He was courageous as a refugee, a soldier, an office manager, and a cancer patient. His mettle shone through in tiny actions—the kind you could easily miss if you weren't paying attention, but I was. He is my hero.

NOBLE QUALITIES

In the summer of 1998, I graduated college and read a biography of Abraham Lincoln called *With Malice Toward None*. The night I finished it, I sat there next to Kirsten with tears streaming down my cheeks. "Did you not know how it was going to end?" she teased me. Since that day I am, without apology, a full-on nerd for anything having to do with Lincoln. His work ethic, management style, fierce determination, and resilience have all been minor obsessions ever since. I even wear a collector's edition Lincoln belt buckle around my waist most days.

We talk so much about him around the house that my children were shocked to learn that Honest Abe had died. "What?" they exclaimed one night as though I had been keeping his death a secret. "When? How?" They wanted the details of his assassination. I filled them in, and the look of terror on their faces made me wonder whether I'd said too much. This past Father's Day I got a card that read, "To my dad, just as cool as Abraham Lincoln." So I guess they're doing OK with the news.

Don't worry; I'm not about to give a history lesson on Abraham Lincoln. I will, however, say this: While the 16th President of the United States achieved outstanding things and was without question a courageous man, what I most admire about him is his practical application of the noble qualities so many of us endeavor to possess—the virtues of the world's greatest religions, on plain display from a man who was nothing if not completely human.

Humility. Patience. Kindness. Accountability. Tolerance. Empathy. Forgiveness.

Few leaders throughout history have so willingly welcomed those that disagreed with them into their inner circle. My personal favorite was his practice of writing but not sending vitriolic letters. Rather than rifle off knee-jerk reactions to those he was upset with, thereby exacerbating the situation, he'd tuck them into his desk drawer and consider whether they ought to be sent. It's almost impossible to fathom in an age of presidential firestorm tweeting sessions. But that's who he was, in theory *and* in practice. He battled melancholia, the crushing blow of losing a child, and the challenge of having a spouse prone to manic-depressive episodes—all while the fate of the nation was in his hands. The magnanimity of the man was never clearer than at the end of the Civil War. He instructed the generals to "let 'em up easy." And they killed him anyway.

The world may not always pat us on the back when we do the right thing, but we know nobility when we see it, and Lincoln was a king. A servant king, but a king nonetheless.

THOSE WHO WENT BEFORE US

We all want to believe that we are the masters of our own destiny. Self-made. Gladiators and goddesses. But we stand on the shoulders of giants. Everything we've ever learned came from those who preceded us, and it is because of them that we know where to direct our aim at all. Heroes epitomize ambition. It is through their example that we become the best version of ourselves.

It doesn't have to be a famous person. Mothers and fathers make great heroes. Bosses. Teachers. Fictional characters. Whatever. What matters is that we connect to our idols as authentic people. We allow them to be less than perfect and reveal themselves to us as fellow travelers in the human race.

I hope I never find out that Lincoln was mean to children or something like that, but even if I do, it won't change the fact that he held his country together throughout a civil war and abolished slavery. Likewise, I will never know what secrets died with my grandfather. I'm not sure he was the greatest parent; patience was never his virtue. I already know that John Daly has a potty mouth and plenty of demons that he wrestles with, but in his company, I find my own demons less daunting. So, yeah, it's important to have heroes.

PART TWO

EVERYTHING ELSE THAT MATTERS

OBJECTS IN THE MIRROR

11.28.76
Day that I was born, right before my parents split
It was hard I know on them
When you're young raising children

As we look back through the looking glass
Visions closer than they appear
Stubbing toes on toys, those days you'll wish were still here
They'll be objects in the mirror

1.28.86
Our eyes glued to school's only television set
No one told us, now we knew
Every dream does not come true

As we look back through the looking glass
Visions closer than they appear
Even when they say the sky above will be clear
There will be objects in the mirror

4.1.2003
The day I said goodbye to my favorite refugee
If he came to us again
Would we even let him in?

5.13.2012
Last day I remember mama acting like herself
When the angels took her home
I was never so alone

As we look back through the looking glass
Visions closer than they appear
When you're holding on to the hope of one more year
We're just objects in the mirror

10.2.17
Terror in Las Vegas and the ghost of Tom Petty
All these big guns in bad hands
Cannot bring back one good man

As we look back through the looking glass
Visions closer than they appear
If fear itself is the only thing we should fear
What of these objects in the mirror?

12.31.17
Surrounded by my family, 12 o'clock on New Year's Eve
Throwing paper on the fire
Nothing else that we require
'Cause a heart with no regrets
Is as good as it can get

As we look back through the looking glass
Visions closer than they appear
There're so many things to be grateful for my dear
All these objects in the mirror
Objects in the mirror

CHAPTER 6
TIME

What follows are a series of reflections and observations about time. To be sure, the science of time is mind-bending. Mind-bending but not something I'm inclined, or knowledgeable enough, to talk about. I'm more fascinated with the 24-hour day and how the heck we're supposed to get work done, raise our kids, meditate, take care of our skin, exercise, eat healthy, stay up on current affairs, practice random acts of kindness, volunteer, and somehow get eight hours of sleep—all while supposedly remembering to smile and live in the moment. It does not seem possible and yet, in fits and starts, it is. I'm willing to bet that the greater understanding we have of time, the more likely we are to make valuable use of the years we are given. And the good news is that none of this requires any aptitude for physics. So, without further ado, here goes.

Time...

...IS NOT, IT TURNS OUT, ON OUR SIDE

Ben Franklin told us not to squander it, and the Rolling Stones claim to have it on their side. But have you seen Mick Jagger lately? He's aged just like the rest of us. Never mind if my editor finds him sexy as all get-out, the man looks older. I think the author of *Poor Richard's Almanac* was closer to the mark: Do not misuse time. You only get so much of it, and once you piss it away, that's all she wrote. No refunds or exchanges. It's why when people reach a ripe old age, they have more regrets about how they spent their time than their money.

Think of it as an accumulation of gold coins bestowed on us at birth. What if over the course of our lifetime we were able to actually see the pile dwindling? Under those circumstances would we be less casual about how easily we dispersed our allotments? Maybe. But unfortunately, that's not how it works, and so we get distracted by shiny things we can hold in our hands while the real gold slips past us.

It's our most precious commodity, and yet there isn't anybody who doesn't waste at least some of it on a daily basis. I've been known to wander the grocery store trying to remember what I went in there to get, and I'm confident there is little to be gained from the minutes I spend observing my nose in the mirror. As to the hours frittered away on the Internet...don't get me started.

The cliché "Everything happens for a reason" comes in handy as a justification for our poor use of time. The boyfriends that didn't work out, the jobs that worked out even less, the nights spent joylessly inebriated or in pursuits so ill-advised we can scarcely remember them without a flush of embarrassment. I gave the better part of 1986 to the video game *Legend of Zelda.* So much energy misapplied in an effort to win the approval of those who were simply not worth it. Sure, it all may be happening *for a reason,* but I'd still rather not miss my flight, if you get my drift. We're over here trying to build a life, and all the while time is thumbing its nose at us. If you're anything like me, you could generate a substantial list of time you'd really like to get back.

And that's not to say that all unfocused time is a waste. Everyone needs to stare off into the distance once in a while, but it's hard to know if we're getting the balance right, and in the meantime the hourglass just keeps running. There are no assurances about tomorrow, so there ends up being a fair amount of pressure on today.

Time doesn't do a little dance for fame or fortune, because it doesn't give a shit. It doesn't much consider the plans (or lack thereof) that we have for ourselves. It's not cruel, just indifferent, like an older sibling we're in awe of. Time is a badass, but it's *not* on our side.

...IS AND IS NOT OF THE ESSENCE

Over the course of writing this book, I lost time on more than a few occasions. I'd miss getting together with friends or a business opportunity because I was busy writing, which frequently amounted to me staring at the computer screen while trying not to get distracted by the barrage of advertisements on *Thesaurus.com*. Sometimes I would tell my kids that I'd be right up to put them to bed, and they would have already fallen asleep before I got there. I'd hear "Cat's in the Cradle" play in my mind, as I left their bedroom having blown my chance to tuck them in. Had I screwed that up? Miscalculated my priorities?

We can't reconstruct the hours and minutes of days gone by, but when I envision life as a novel that's still being written, it helps me keep the whole time-management thing in perspective. I think of the chapters like years, pages like months, and paragraphs like days. When you get all the way down to the individual words, they're akin to the incidental stuff we do, like, say, taking a pee when we get up in the morning—essential but not eventful. Looking at it this way, I feel less anxious about the time inevitably wasted, because in this context not every moment needs to be *the* moment. It's all part of the bigger picture.

The fact that the story is still being written is important, too, as it's easy to stop creating a future for ourselves once we arrive at middle age. There's a weird perception that whatever dreams we had early on should have materialized by the age of 40; a myth that whoever we were going to become, we should already be and that, by this point, we'd better have sorted everything out. It doesn't make sense, of course, because there are lots of late bloomers among us (*raises hand*).

Upon realizing that there is more time behind us than in front of us, we may find ourselves reaching back toward whatever the best moments of our past were. Maybe it was college, or maybe some period in our early 30s when we were kicking ass and feeling limitless possibilities. When my long-time band the Sixers broke up, I spent a few years paralyzed by the notion that I'd never again make music as good as that which I had already made. It wasn't until I moved beyond that idea that I was able to conceive of a bright future for myself. If we're not careful, we can get stuck and end up pining away for what *was* instead of writing an exciting new installment. I don't want that for myself, and I don't want that for you.

The takeaway in all this is that it's important to actively believe in the next chapter, because even when we're not paying attention, our biography is being written. The saga unfolds regardless. Some of it is beyond our control, but much of it is ours to shape, and that's the stuff we want to concentrate on. And we need to do so without getting preoccupied by all the loose ends. No sense expecting closure on every subplot. I haven't seen at least half the people who attended my wedding since the day I got married. I don't know what they're up to, and I'm guessing I may never know. What I do know is this: Some parts of our life will be of more consequence than others, and since we can't be sure which will be which, best to make it all count as much as possible.

Our time here is finite. We need to create space for the things that are important to us, and when we believe otherwise, we are kidding ourselves. If we want to have a good marriage, we'd better schedule occasion for romance. If we want our kids to know they matter, we'll have to be as available to them as we are to our pals at the golf course. If we want to be great at our profession, we'll need to do the heavy lifting, even if it means falling behind on our favorite Netflix shows. Why didn't they tell us it would be so hard to make these choices? Maybe we should be teaching children the inestimable value of time right now while they're young. Maybe they'll regret less...or maybe not.

...WAITS FOR NO MAN

Am I the same person I was as a boy because some of me remains the same, or am I a different person because some of me has changed? It's got to be both, but if you think too hard about it, it'll make your brain hurt.

Aside from the actor Paul Rudd, everyone ages. And in that life span we either take a few shots or we don't, but time isn't going to hold on while we decide. So when they say, "Time waits for no man," I think what they are getting at in layman's terms is that (a) our bodies will one day turn into raisins and (b) this is not a rehearsal. There's a twofold meaning behind the adage. Let's start with the aging, because I have a number of newly sprouted grey hairs and a case of rosacea that are just begging to be considered.

Many friends of mine spend a lot of time trying to look younger than they are. I kind of get it. I do keep a bottle of Rogaine in the medicine cabinet, and personally I'd love to have a thick mane of hair like I did when I was in college. The problem is that I only remember to use the stuff once in a while because I'm not sure I think it actually works. Plus, who can devote their morning to fussing over it all anyway? My hairline (and not me) is the one losing the battle. Same with my flakey complexion—no cream or moisturizer is ever going to erase four decades of living. I've read that our skin regenerates every 27 days, but I haven't been carded in years, so I'm skeptical of that too.

We report on people's appearances though. *She looks older. He's gained weight.* Or maybe if we're feeling generous, we say that a person *looks good for their age.* We note how they've changed. Sometimes we mean it in a positive way, other times the reverse. When I'm on the road, people don't always remember their manners and they'll come up to me and say that I look tired. First of all, I *am* tired, but that's beside the point. How does a person who says things like that have any friends in real life?

And again, I'll ask, am I or am I not the same person regardless of how old I appear to be? Does time put those lines on my face by itself, or is it a series of decisions consciously and unconsciously made along the way that speeds the process? More important, why are we so concerned? That ought to be the question we're asking ourselves. It's not our love handles that matter, it's what we've done while our pals were getting facials.

•·················•·················•

And as for the hourglass's role in reminding us that this is not a drill...

What if the purpose of the passing years is to break us down until we're ready to die? Now I know that might sound morbid, but I've always found it motivating. A little angel (or devil) on my shoulder telling me to "Get moving, boy—make your mark!" It's like we start out intrepid, then by middle school get nervous about what our peers will think of us; as young adults we recover some of our pluckiness, striking out on our own, but by adulthood we've all watched way too much news to not find the world at least partially terrifying. If there is a silver lining to the end of life, it's got to be the relief from pain and fear. So in a sense, maybe we're racing against a clock of how much torment our hearts can endure. I think this way, but it's possible that I'm just projecting my emotional baggage onto you. I do that sometimes.

My point, though, is that it's lonesome when people we love pass away. Once we've survived a certain amount of tragedy, it's hard not to be afraid. Life is scary. And death, in all its finality, is the cutoff most of us have chosen to ignore even though it has been hurtling toward us since the moment we were born. But there's nothing like a deadline to let a person know how long they can procrastinate. So, in lieu of having to acknowledge our mortality, procrastinate we do.

I didn't stop cramming for tests when I graduated college. The sleepless nights and last-minute panic are a part of my DNA. The delay of the awkward conversation; the belated birthday gift; the home improvement project that never seems to get done; the much-neglected dentist appointment (do you ever give your teeth such a thorough going over as when you're scheduled for a cleaning?). The countless amount of times I've walked on stage wishing I had practiced harder or started prepping a little earlier. I'm always anxious when I wait too long to do a thing, but that doesn't stop me from putting it off.

When we pretend the final due date doesn't exist, we operate under the false assumption that there will always be more time. Instead of potentially making the wrong choice, we make no choice and suffer the consequences. We miss our chance to perfect the art of the 89.5 by needing to get a perfect grade.

This is why when the band Train asked me to fill in for their lead singer, Pat Monahan, who had lost his voice, I agreed even though I wasn't sure I was up to the task. Pat is an incredible vocalist with an epic range that eclipses my own by several octaves. They contacted me only hours before the show. I would be playing to 3,000 of their most die-hard fans, and I wasn't all that familiar with the material, but I also knew it was a one shot deal, and a chance to impress my kids, so I walked on stage and sang "Drops of Jupiter" and "Calling All Angels" to the best of my ability. I didn't hit all the notes, but I had a hell of a time.

If we devote our energy to getting everything right, we might be ignoring the fact that *done is beautiful*; better to do a thing imperfectly than not do a thing at all.

...DOES NOT, UNDER ANY CIRCUMSTANCES, HEAL ALL WOUNDS

In spite of the many clever aphorisms about time, I'm sure that it does not, in fact, heal *all* wounds. For the most part, nothing is ever the same once it's broken. Case in point: I rolled my ankle on some stairs in 2007; after that, forget about capture the flag—I could sprain it walking to the bathroom. And I'm talking about psychological and emotional wounds as well. I'm pretty sure my seventh-grade girlfriend told me she "just needed some time" the day she broke up with me.

Google and other corporations continue to invest untold billions trying to somehow prolong life, but it's a fart in a hurricane. From cryogenics to the best health care on the planet, the attempt to obtain more time has no guarantees. "It's not the years in your life, it's the life in your years," we say. In theory I love it, but then try telling that to a 12-year-old with cancer. It doesn't hold up.

I met Julianna Edel while playing at a hospital in Hackensack, NJ. She hadn't been able to attend the performance because she was too susceptible to infection to be around the other patients. I was told if I wore a sanitary mask, I could go see her. She was lovely. Her smile was radiant. I sang for Julianna and she played her violin for me. I started making plans to have her sit in with the band. It was not to be. She was gone within months.

Time might heal some wounds, but it sure doesn't heal all wounds.

...IS, LEST WE FORGET, RELATIVE

"It goes fast," the neighbor says to me as we shake our heads in disbelief. It's the first day of school and the bus has just pulled away. Eight years we've been meeting at the end of the driveway, but it feels like eight days. Somehow, though, it also seems like eight lifetimes. So many tours between then and now. So many nights in strange hotels and days spent traveling. So many dishes done. So much screen time. I snap myself out of the daydream. I'm going to be picked up for a business trip in less than an hour and I haven't packed a thing. Sound familiar?

The next 57 minutes will fly by in a blur. No matter how quickly I jam clothes in a bag, or food in a mouth, it's unlikely that I'll be ready when the driver arrives. Being on time has always been a struggle for me. Arriving within 15 minutes of when I'm supposed to be there is a major achievement. But for the prompt people of the world, that's a disgrace. It's rude, no doubt, but I don't think I realized how annoying it was until I started raising a teenager who is quite incapable of being on time herself. For her we wait and wait...and wait. It boils my blood, but I refuse to accept that the 15 minutes she keeps me waiting is equivalent to the 15 minutes I keep everyone else waiting. How's that for self-awareness?

If you've ever doubted the theory of time's relativity, I encourage you to consider the difference between five minutes spent making love versus five minutes battling a stomach flu. One is euphoric and over before you know it, while the other drags on ad infinitum.

One of the greatest moments of my life was standing on stage in Washington, DC, at the legendary 9:30 Club for a fourth encore. It seemed the people would never stop clapping, and when I'd go to take the microphone, they would cheer even louder. Eventually, I was in tears. I was too young, then, to know how much poise it would take to be present for that moment, and like smoke through my hands, it passed far too quickly. The buzz wore off, though I'm grateful for the recollection. That was time at its fastest.

By contrast, there are holiday parties that fall under the umbrella of obligatory social engagements. These are the sorts of environments that introverts like me dread. I get energy through time spent in solitude. At some point I hit a wall where my face can no longer smile, my patience is gone, and I have to remove myself from a setting before I turn to dust. I happen to have married a woman who could not be more of a contrast to me in this respect. Kirsten is an extrovert through and through. She gains steam with every new person she meets. And when we go out, she does her best to meet *all* the people. There are times when we're preparing to leave somewhere, and I'll say, "You about ready to go, hon?"

"Yeah, maybe a few more minutes."

"Not for me. I'll meet you in the bushes outside if I have to, but I'm done."

Then as we're exiting the gathering, I will actually see her spot someone across the room. Not just someone we haven't said goodbye to, but someone we don't even know. Those last 10 minutes, while she's introducing herself to her new friend so that we can say goodbye to him or her, will creep by at a pace that is reminiscent of a sloth crossing the Grand Canyon. It has been this way for years, but what are you going to do? Time is relative.

...IS, BY THE BY, THE STUFF LIFE IS MADE OF

I watch the clock when I'm hurting, just to know that part of what has happened is behind me. I read somewhere that if we live to be 80 years old, we will take approximately 650 million breaths. Will we remember any of them?

Every once in a while, the good moments do manage to sink in. You realize you're in the midst of making one of the best memories you will ever have. It's then that time makes the most sense. We can ponder it all we like, but in those brief periods what's clearest is the directive F. Scott Fitzgerald gave us in *The Curious Case of Benjamin Button*: "I hope you live a life you're proud of. If you find that you're not, I hope you have the courage to start all over again."

RIGHT THERE WITH YOU

When you're lost, worn out, and weary
And this life weighs you down like a stone
There are no stars to guide you and no one to hold
But there in the darkness, you're not alone

Where there is pain, there you will find me
Where there is love, I'll be there too
I will be right there with you

When grace, she feels like a memory
An embrace that has long left you cold
Oh, when your spirit has ceased to be hopeful
You will be carried, you're not alone

Where there is pain, there you will find me
Where there is love, I'll be there too
When you're searching for peace, when you're down on your knees

I will be right there with you
I will be right there with you
I will be right there with you

CHAPTER 7
HEALTH

"Still drink two days a week?" Doctor Bob asks me. I was either lying or 17 years old when I must have last answered the question, so I tell him the truth.

"Closer to four...*ish*," my guilty eyes focus on my shoelaces.

"OK. One to two drinks on those nights?" he looks up at me over his glasses. I give him a meek smile and inform him that three drinks is probably closer to the mark, at which point he takes off his glasses, widens his gaze a little and says, "Never more than four though?"

I could see where this was going. With all the gravity I could muster, I responded that yes, I had more than four drinks a few times a month. I thought of trying to qualify it with explanations about my artist lifestyle, but the words sounded lame even before they left my mouth. And let's face it, wine for the kids' bath time was as much a part of this as any celebrity gala I was attending.

"That's too much."

The news didn't improve from there. Somewhere between my prostate exam and having my Austin Powers–like chest shaved for a cardiogram, I began to feel my 40s acutely. *How much do you exercise*? About 25 minutes every other week. *Do you eat well*? Not really. *Are you stressed*? Of course, isn't everybody? *Do you feel healthy*? Kind of.

●··················●··················●

I want you to take everything I'm about to say on the topic of health with a big ol' grain of salt. It's one of those areas in life that I know is very important and yet can't bring myself to zero in on beyond a begrudging jog or occasional plate of greens. I do not have all the answers. And I'm not going to judge your habits, so I'd prefer that you not judge mine, but like any Monday morning quarterback, just because I don't play the game doesn't mean I don't have an opinion as to how it should be played.

When it comes to health, I hold three beliefs dearly. First, it's different for everyone. This is something that no book on the subject wants to admit because that would require an acceptance that whatever diet, regime, or philosophy they are selling might not work for the person reading it.

Second, I subscribe to Joe Kennedy's maxim, "After you've done your best, then the hell with it." A concerted effort at pristine health might make sense on paper, but we shouldn't do so at the expense of our day-to-day peace of mind. Joy is medicine, too, and eating a bucket of popcorn at the movies is sometimes what's called for. Still, the better we feel, the less we have to consider how we feel. And no one knows this more than a sick person. But for those of us in reasonable health, it's not realistic nor desirable to spend all of our time fretting about perfect health.

Last, physical and mental health are inexorably inter-twined, and taking care of either is an expensive business. It is through a spin of the roulette wheel that we are born into economic stations that, in many cases, dictate the access we will have to health care. Put simply, a lot of people can't afford a doctor.

It's bad enough that my buddy doesn't have the financial means to take his daughter to the orthopedist for her broken wrist, but it's equally jarring to imagine what happens when we can't swing the necessary treatment for psychological trauma. We are only now beginning to understand the costs of neglecting our mental health. One out of every four people on the planet will suffer from mental or neurological disorders at some point in their life, and we can't even get aspirin to certain parts of the globe. So what can we do?

FOOD

When we were kids, we were told that the four food groups were essential. Sloppy joe was on equal footing with the as yet unheard of kale. My mom and sister put cottage cheese on everything. Count Chocula was a popular breakfast cereal for kids, and we had no awareness of gluten. We microwaved most things, even though the outcome produced food that was equal parts scorching hot and freezing cold. A hot dog in the microwave is still to this day a risky culinary gamble. Margarine was good and butter was bad, until butter was good and margarine was bad. Come to think of it, do we know which one is good now? Probably neither. My dad used to cook us a meal each week that consisted of baked beans, creamed corn, and macaroni and cheese. The visual was uncanny.

Our understanding of the human diet has changed a lot since then. We no longer hold processed foods up as the hallmark of convenience. The supermarket is now filled with buzzwords like *free range* and *non-GMO*. But one thing that hasn't changed is that we still tend to eat what we can whip up without too much trouble. If I'm really busy, I just put cheese on bread and then take a bite of a pickle with each mouthful so that I don't have to go through the whole process of making a sandwich. No judgment, remember.

Not many of us have the time and resources to hire a cook or make intricate meals using fresh local ingredients. We rely on our grocery stores and restaurants to do right by us, and while some do, many do not. I guess my point is that this should matter to us. Where we source our food is as important as what our food is.

An apple a day won't always keep the doctor away, but as long as it's not covered in pesticides, it's probably going to help. Food may be the best medicine we have. More whole grains, less meat; less sugar, more water. I recently read that a plant-based diet of leafy greens and vegetables is the key to optimum health, but if you're asking me if I'd rather have a salad or a chicken parmesan grinder, I've got to go with the meat, cheese, and carbs.

Our body will tell us what it needs. No one wakes up after

crushing late night Big Macs and feels good. It just doesn't happen. But when we pay attention to our innate feedback loop, we're more apt to know what our system requirements are. And it's not only the type of food we eat but the quantity. This is where my hypocrisy-meter reaches a fever pitch. Portion control is my arch nemesis.

Somewhere along the way I went from being a kid who was "a good eater" to being a man who consumes calories like a sumo wrestler. I stress eat. The food is the drug. Some of you out there know exactly what I'm talking about. I have a high metabolism, so it doesn't show much, but I can probably take down more tacos than most guys in the NFL. Pizza is my favorite. I don't see it as a meal but, rather, as a challenge. Thin crust New York–style, Chicago deep dish, Stouffer's French bread, you name it. I love them all. Never met a pizza I didn't like. Even when it's bad, it's great.

My father is this way with wine. I mentioned to him last Thanksgiving that I sometimes felt as though I didn't have an off switch when it came to eating. My dad looked up from his bowl of chardonnay and said, "Not me, sonny, you just have to stop before you're full." *Oh really, Dad, is that all? How zen.* Keep in mind this is a man whom I've seen bolt across the kitchen with a tear in his eye in order to stop a glass of white wine with a bug in it from being poured into the sink. But now I find myself perhaps drinking more than I should, so who am I to talk? I'll say this though: I don't know anyone who is a better person *because* they drink.

EXERCISE

I know some people are addicted to working out, but I am not one of them. If I didn't set a New Year's resolution every year and make tick marks in my journal, I'm certain I would not exercise. I share this with friends who often commiserate and then proceed to tell me about the half marathon they're running next weekend. The best part of any physical activity, as far as I'm concerned, is when it's over.

It was easier when we were little. My friends and I would spend countless hours outdoors playing games like tag and Wiffle ball. I'd leave in the morning and get called back in only for dinnertime. I rode my bike to school, too, and if any one of us had ever used a helmet, we would have been teased mercilessly for doing so. It was a sturdier time then. Kids were allowed a lot more room to move around. Not that it was always a good thing.

I can remember running from the cops after my neighbor vandalized the nearby golf course. The police chased us kids through backyards and shortcuts until we finally got away. Now *that* was a workout! These days, cell phones with tracking devices aside, if you see a 13-year-old walking alone, even in broad daylight, it's cause for alarm. *Why is she by herself? What is that boy up to?* The pendulum has swung so far.

Technology seems to have made us more sedentary. We get excited about apps that count our steps or track our heartbeats, but it's these little distractions in our pockets that curbed the unsupervised outdoor time in the first place. Cell phones are like the cigarettes of our generation. "We didn't know they were bad for us," we will say someday, as if constantly putting a little box of radiation up to your head was ever going to end well.

When I first became an adult, I tried to stay active, but I lost interest by the age of 30, probably earlier—too many other things to do. And when you're not accustomed to exercise, your chances of getting injured go way up. Jammed fingers, pulled muscles. I didn't want to risk it.

I worked out with my friend Taylor a few months ago. He's fit. He asked me how many push-ups a day I do, and I asked him what the hell kind of question that was. He then decided I should start by doing six push-ups, six sit-ups, and six Russian twists (a little move where you sit on the

floor with a five-pound weight and angle back and forth).
Six struck me as too low a number, so I insisted that I do
a whopping 10 of each. Do you know what happened? I
sprained my thumb. I knew I shouldn't have exercised.

• · · · · · · · · · · · · · · · · • · · · · · · · · · · · · · · · · •

The one exercise I do enjoy is sex.

Sex is a natural human drive, like hunger or thirst. It
can lower our risk of heart disease, blood pressure, and
stress level, all while improving the function of our prostate, bladder, and immune system, but somewhere along
the way we moralized it to be something naughty. A topic
we're not supposed to mention in polite company. We've
built a culture where sexuality is so taboo, we rarely feel at
ease discussing it. But we're doing ourselves a disservice in
this regard. No wonder we have a growing population of
people addicted to pornography. We're letting the bad guys
tell the story and not weighing in with a healthy alternative.

Sometimes folks see me with my four daughters and
make jokes about "locking them up," "getting them to a
convent," or even "feeling bad for me." For years I would
smile and play along, until one day I noticed the girls were
watching. Being comfortable with your sexuality is one of

the greatest gifts life could offer, so why wouldn't I want that for my children? Why was I indulging strangers in perpetuating a stereotype that sexual pleasure is uniquely male and not something for women to enjoy just as much? I hated that idea. There is already too much emphasis on teaching girls how not to get assaulted (watch what you wear, don't let the guys think you're easy, don't walk alone at night) and not enough focus on teaching boys that it's never OK to pressure another person into doing things that they don't want to do. There are parts of the world where women are still treated as second-class citizens. I believe that's wrong, and I'd never want my daughters to think there was any ambiguity as to where I stood on that.

The talk is a thing of the past. What we need now is *the dialogue*. It's not always easy to know what to say, but we've got to get comfortable saying something.

One night while putting my 8-year-old to bed, she asked where babies come from. Ah, that old chestnut. My wife and I exchanged furtive glances and gave her a vague answer about a man and woman conceiving. Her face crinkled in confusion.

"But how does it get into your stomach?"

I sighed. There was no skirting this one. "A man puts his penis in a woman's vagina. Then the baby grows inside the woman and comes back out of the vagina."

Her eyes grew as big as saucers.

"Nothing to be scared of, honey."

The next morning she told us in no uncertain terms that if that was how babies came out, she wanted none of it. And that made us all laugh.

DOCTORS

Going to the doctor sucks. Even when I'm feeling great, I'm worried that they'll find something wrong. Every time I get a headache, I suspect that it might be a disease causing my brain to swell. On a hypochondria scale of 1 to 10, I posture as a 7, but I'm definitely an 8, maybe even a 9. I used to pass out at the sight of a needle, and I think I still would if my pride would allow it. The irony is that I see more doctors now than ever before: primary care, podiatrist, dermatologist, optometrist, naturopath, dentist, and on we go. With four kids and a wife who is as prone to thinking she's sick as I am, we spend a lot of time and money at the doctor's office. Kirsten has had them run so many random tests on her in recent years that I thought I might get her a gift certificate to Quest Diagnostics next Christmas. But on balance we're both healthy, and no one is forcing us to go. So why bother?

Because wellness visits are easier than sick visits. Prevention is better than cure, and if my going to see the gastroenterologist increases the chances of watching my grandkids grow up someday, I'm in.

When I came to after having my first colonoscopy, I rang for the nurse immediately and asked for something to write with. As Tom Petty once said, "If the muse comes to visit you and you don't write it down, that's just ruuuuude." Keeping a journal has always kept me sane, and waking up in a hospital with your johnny gown hanging open doesn't change that. I wrote down a single sentence.

On the doctor's table we are all the same.

That made me feel better.

SPIRITUAL WELL-BEING

I don't want to fight about any of this. I don't care what religion you are or are not. It doesn't matter to me because I'm confident our ability to attend to the soul has nothing to do with which team we choose to identify with or how often we go to church (apologies to all my Catholic friends for whom I know that's disappointing news). I've met healthy atheists and plenty of ailing religious zealots.

I once had a couple approach me after a concert to tell me that, although they enjoyed my music, I would not be going to heaven. I thought they must be kidding, but the sympathetic smile they both wore told me otherwise. *Ah, so you're God*, I thought to myself. *Funny, I never pictured you living in Tampa, Florida, dressed in floral print.*

They were responding to my lyrics. I've been known to raise questions of faith from time to time. Doubts. And apparently my spiritual exploration didn't align with their own. I was headed, in their not-so-humble opinion, to a life of eternal damnation. I smiled and tried to seem less irked than I was.

The healthiest people I know all have some kind of spiritual ballast. It doesn't matter how we arrive there, just that we arrive there. For some that means giving back. It's impossible to help others without helping ourselves. I also have friends who swear by meditation, but every time I try to meditate, I give up or fall asleep. Meditating properly is right there on the to-do list with getting my golf score below 90 and growing a vegetable garden. I'm not there yet, but that doesn't mean it's not an awesome place to be.

I choose to pray. I focus on the most loving frequency I can find on any given day, and I pray for whomever I think needs it, including myself. It's basically a matter of sending good vibrations into the universe. What could we possibly lose in doing so? Worst-case scenario, it doesn't do a damn thing. But in the event that it does work? Well, let's just say that's the easiest money in the bank you'll ever make.

Spiritual well-being is a personal journey.

REST

E.J. Cossman said, "The best bridge between despair and hope is a good night's sleep." I can't remember the last time I got eight hours. I always love it when the doctor tells me to get lots of rest and drink plenty of fluids; even though the two directives are at cross-purposes—what with getting up to go to the bathroom and all—it's nice to be told that it's OK to take a break.

There have been times as a parent and touring musician when I have barely slept for days on end. Panic sets in. The simplest tasks start to feel insurmountable. I find myself snapping in situations that wouldn't normally get my dander up. I yelled at my bandmate the other day for eating Greek yogurt in my presence. I do hate the smell of it, but the punishment didn't fit the crime. I hadn't slept much.

It all comes down to energy, and when the brain gets

too exhausted, it starts giving us bad data. Through tired eyes everything looks overwhelming. When we're rested, the opposite seems true.

In the event we do get sick, the burden falls on those around us to care for us. Often, it's those we love the most, and there is nothing more taxing on a relationship than the dynamics that arise in illness. This is why we need to learn to rest.

• · · · · · · · · · · · · · · · · · • · · · · · · · · · · · · · · · · · •

I'm not sure if I'll ever sleep again the way I used to. It's doubtful. I don't know to what degree I'll get my eating habits reeled in or become an Ironman triathlete. I do know that I've chosen a life that's made brainwork and soulwork easier than rest. And that's OK.

Our health is not to be worn as a badge of honor. It's not something to be flaunted in the faces of those who feel its absence. Good health is its own reward. I may not treat my body like a temple, but as with my own home, I'm grateful for its gifts even when it's a mess. Now if only they'll release a study that says eating pizza every day is the road to ideal health. Wouldn't that be nice?

EASY MONEY

If somewhere there is easy money, I haven't found it yet
The dollars I've made throwing some sort of shade,
Were always a source of regret
Now I am a rich man, I know that I am, but sometimes I don't feel that way
Like just when you make a few bucks for yourself,
There's some other bill to be paid

And it's cash on the barrelhead,
Time out of mind,
Feels like we're coming in hot
When it comes to easy money
My hands might shake, but my heart does not
Easy money

I have a friend, we don't talk anymore,
Because somehow I think that he thought
I had a stash of unlimited cash, when he told me he couldn't be bought

That's good 'cause I wouldn't know where to begin
And friendship ain't something you buy
And if business is just business
Well, I don't care to be that kind of guy
Easy money, easy money
Easy money, come lay on my door

Well, I don't need a diamond or mother of pearl
'Cause I've got a wife and four beautiful girls
But if someday the gods of distraction decide
That I was a pretty good guy, bring that easy money

Easy money
Easy money
Easy money, come lay on my door...

CHAPTER 8:
WORK

Work gets a bad rap.

The words "I've got to work" are usually delivered with a groan and the inference that one would rather be doing anything else. Somehow, I've always loved it though. The idea of completing tasks appeals to my OCD.

I understand the aversions. It's hard to consider the benefits of a job when you don't feel you have a choice in the matter. For many of us, we just know there are bills to pay and if we don't go to work, we can't pay them.

There are times when it genuinely sucks no matter who

you are or what you do; if not because of the job itself, then at least because, with the law of averages, not every day can be a good day. And once you've realized that your precious minutes are, in fact, precious, who wants to spend them doing something they don't care about? Certainly not those who subscribe to the old adage "Do what you love, and you'll never have to work a day in your life." But I think Adam J. Kurtz's revision of that idea is closer to the truth anyway: "Do what you love, and you'll work super fucking hard all the time with no separation or any boundaries and also take everything extremely personally." Being passionate about what you do can be a 24-7 enterprise. But everything I've ever done in my life that I'm proud of began with butterflies and took plenty of elbow grease.

The thing is, everybody works. Most Americans live paycheck to paycheck, but even if we do manage to become financially liberated, we'll probably still want a job for the sake of our own sanity because *doing nothing is exhausting.* Nowhere to go and no clear purpose has been the ruin of many a wealthy parent's son or daughter. A person can only watch so much TV before starting to question their existence; and although there are plenty of productive outlets for our time when we're not working, you could argue that if we're doing something productive, it's a kind of a career unto itself. Regardless, most of us will, at some point in our lifetime, seek gainful employment.

While the work we do each day does not always define us, the way that we approach it does. And other than sleep, it's what we'll be doing with the majority of our time here on earth, so it pays to be as particular as we can afford to be about the jobs we choose. Our happiness, or failure to be happy in this regard, may be the difference between a life we enjoy and one that makes us miserable.

Of course, I have to be careful when discussing this particular subject because, on balance, I really enjoy what I do for a living. I'm well aware that anyone struggling with their occupation may not want to hear a peep from a guy whose job description includes the words *occasional rock star*. I assure you, though, it wasn't always this way.

STARTING SOMEWHERE

I graduated college at the top of my class with high honors, a member of the Golden Key International Honour Society. That's right, *honour* with a 'u.' Four months later, when I was living with my parents and still had no idea what I would be doing with the rest of my life, I got my first call back for a job interview. I asked my mom for help ironing my shirt and scratched out notes on a piece of paper about the company I was going to be interviewing with. "A MUSIC COMPANY" I put in all CAPS as though it was something I might forget.

I also wrote down a minimum base salary and promised myself I would, under no circumstances, accept less. At the end of my interview, compensation had not yet been discussed, so I inquired as to what the pay was. "Six dollars an hour" I was informed. I searched his face for some indication that he was joking. Not finding any, I tried to hide my disappointment. This was low even by the standards of 1998. Biding my time and having belied my shock long enough, I countered with, "Are there benefits?"

"No." He was unapologetic.

"I'll take it." So was I.

●·················●·················●

That's the thing about a job. We're always happy to get them. It's when we have to do the labor we've been hired to do that we get a little grouchy. We start thinking about the fat cash at the end of the rainbow and aren't always up for the many hours it takes to get there. I've stood on enough stages with drunk people ignoring me or telling me to "shut up and sing" to know that there's no such thing as an overnight success. It's tempting to imagine an easier life in which less is asked of us and whatever we've already done is recognized as sufficient, but I've never found that to be the case. I used to believe that if I rowed hard enough, at some point the boat might glide on its own; 20-plus years in and I'm still waiting for the part where I coast.

Even after we work long, hard days, the return doesn't always feel worth the investment. So we lament our station and crave more leisure time. We spout off to anyone who will listen about the unreasonable expectations and demands put upon us by our employers. And on occasion we're absolutely right. There are intolerable bosses who lack management skills and are quick to take their employees for granted. What's more, sometimes we need the employment so badly that we're willing to tolerate poor treatment or menial tasks that fail to nourish our spirit and fall well below our capabilities.

While we can't make all the unfortunate rules of the game go away, we can decide how best to react to them. Sometimes this includes quitting, but just as often it means sticking around and making do with what's in front of us. Leaving a soul-sucking job in a blaze of glory might feel amazing in the moment, but it will not pay the rent. And ideally this should be considered *before* telling our boss to "take this job and shove it."

COWORKERS

Getting along with others is one of the biggest obstacles we are likely to face in our occupations. Think kindergarten rules. There are plenty of fancy business schools that will complicate the message in order to promote their services, but in the end our ability to contribute our God-given gifts while harnessing the talents of the team is what's at stake. Everyone who has ever accomplished anything in the course of history has had to surmount this same challenge. So how did they do it? What are the best and worst practices when it comes to those we work with?

To answer these questions, I've gone back through my own lifetime of coworkers. Together we achieved several victories, and at other times blundered in our execution. We resolved conflicts, even when it required compromise, but also periodically let our lesser instincts get the better of us. At its very best, there were marvelous days when everyone in the room felt appreciated. That's always the goal. But let me start by telling you about the first guy who ever wanted to fire me.

WHAT DOESN'T WORK

"You've got a silver tongue, Kellogg," my boss Patrick said to me on my third week as a sales associate for Brooks Pharmacy. I think he meant it as an insult, judging by his tone of voice, but being 16 and a bit of a wise guy, I decided to take it as a compliment.

"Thanks, Pat."

Patrick was 25 years my senior and had been working for Brooks for more than three years when he hired me. Before giving me the job, he had asked with no ambiguity whatsoever if I would be available on weekends and after school. I told him I would be, then proceeded to join the school play and start dating Kirsten, at which point I informed him I wouldn't be.

"I thought you could do weekends?" he pleaded, the betrayal evident in his voice.

"Yeah, just not Fridays or Saturdays, and only on some Sundays. I suppose I could...uh...," I trailed off.

My coworkers consisted of a few other high school kids who were as inattentive to the work as I was, and some much older employees who, I now realize, desperately needed the employment I so casually disrespected. It wasn't that I was trying to be difficult or unpleasant in any way, quite the opposite. I just wanted the job to be more glamorous than it inherently was. I got into the habit of greeting customers by saying, "Welcome to Brooks, where you'll love what we do for you!" which I'm still not sure to this day is one of their actual slogans. People loved it—or seemed to love it. They'd smile, and I'd help them find what they were looking for. Underneath it, though, I didn't care if I stayed or went, and I suspect that was clear to everyone.

One day Patrick called me in to tell me I was on probation. It sounded serious. It turned out he'd been watching my register closely, and it had been coming in "over" on every shift. This meant there was too much money in the till at the end of the day. I laughed in his face and made a crack about helping the company's bottom line, at which point he asked me to clean the employee bathroom.

If I knew where Patrick was now, I'd like to shake his hand and thank him for giving me my first job. I'd like to apologize for making his life harder than it needed to be. I was immature and that was to be expected, I suppose, but also, I misunderstood him. I took him to be another authority figure telling me what to do. I felt like rebellion was the appropriate response, when a little gratitude and deference would have been the classier move. I can only imagine he viewed me as an entitled kid who shouldn't have been given the gig in the first place. After I quit the job to focus on whatever else I was up to, I popped back in there for years until they tore it down. The older members of the staff that worked there never changed. If they only knew how much respect I have for them now.

•·················•·················•

I began my post-collegiate professional career selling tickets in an 8-by-8 kiosk at a mall. This was the job for which I had "negotiated" my six pretax dollars for every 60 minutes of service. Lunch breaks were a half hour. Unpaid. There were days I had to jump out of the sandwich line because I knew I wouldn't make it back in time to resume my shift if I stayed on. Returning to the kiosk hungry, I'd be chastised by a girl I worked with named Tina. "Why don't you pack a bagged lunch like me?" she'd say as though she was some kind of wise old sage. It was true she brought her midday sustenance from home. She would eat in the corner of our box during her downtime and consume the most pungent foods known to man. Tuna salad. Boiled onions. Deviled eggs with sardines. Garlic hummus and cheese soup. Adding insult to injury, her hygiene game wasn't totally on point. She did not wear deodorant. Common ground was elusive, and with each passing day in the booth, my spirits flagged.

Tina's lack of consideration for our close quarters was surreal to me, and yet I never once took the time to broach the subject with her or my office manager. My sense of smell was besieged, and I was *hangry,* but how could she have known? Still, I hated her for it, and I suspect she didn't think much of me either. We probably could have worked it out, but my primary focus was to escape her malodorous company and the captivity of the shopping mall.

I plotted my next moves, making myself indispensable to the company by writing memos on how we could increase profits and improve our customers' experience. It was all a bit over-the-top given the fact that I was still operating from a glorified newsstand, but it worked, and before long I was moved over to the main office. With the promotion came a sizable 13 percent raise ($6.75 an hour, woo-hoo) and the title "assistant *to* the publicist"—never to be confused with "assistant publicist." In lieu of a decent wage for my tireless efforts, a stronger title would have been an easy enough feather in the cap to grant me, but I think my boss was afraid to recognize my work for fear that it would in some way diminish his own. It's hard to respect anyone who keeps their hand on your head, but the cream does rise to the top, and eventually these sorts of people seal their own fate. No one wants to work for a tyrant. I soon grew restless in my new spot at the publicity desk, and it was only a matter of months before I asked to be moved again.

I was like a squirrel gathering nuts. I learned every position the company had and ultimately landed as the assistant talent buyer for the whole operation, where I found myself reporting to Jordi Herold. Cut from the same cloth as the legendary promoter Bill Graham, Jordi was a kind of home-spun, folksy dreamer who was not afraid to lose money from time to time so long as he did it in style. I learned a hell of lot sitting next to him that year, and his tutelage more than balanced out the meager wages I was being paid. Eccentric, intelligent, and wonderful, he was preparing to retire and grooming me to take over for him. He was the best boss I ever had, but still, I wanted to be playing music, not promoting it, and before long, it became clear to me that my days as a promoter were numbered. I surmised that if I couldn't be happy working for him, I'd never be happy working for anyone, so in the spring of 2001, I became an entrepreneur.

Twenty-four years old, engaged, and without the faintest idea of how I would be paying for the life that lay ahead, I set out in the world with a singular idea: *Do work that matters to you.*

WHAT DOES WORK

Knowing why I work and what I'm working toward is what gets me out of bed on the coldest of mornings when I am dead tired, discouraged, and ready to throw in the towel. It's what inspires me to keep going when I'm lost in a piece of writing, accompanied by an ever-present sense of doubt as to whether or not I will even be able to finish the project. It's what causes me to seek out kindred spirits who share my vision and manage the job with strange bedfellows when necessary. If we understand our motivations and those of our coworkers, we have a much better chance of building meaningful relationships and tapping into the strengths of those around us.

My favorite wins have all occurred with people who also possessed my predilection for teamwork. The killer review, the standing ovation, the big paycheck, the well-timed opportunity, the hard-won admiration of a peer—all by-products of a group effort. It comes down to believing that it really does take a village, and that the village is not solely comprised of perfect people doing a perfect job.

Imagine, if you will, walking into a room and treating everyone with the exact same amount of consideration regardless of what they could do for you. Can you? Neither can I. I've almost forgotten what it's like to function without a pecking order. But we can't all be quarterbacks, because there's no way to score without the rest of the team. By those standards, is any one position really more important than another?

If we understand what everyone in the organization is bringing to the table and how it helps with the end game, we're more apt to build a culture of appreciation. Plus, the way we treat those who can seemingly do nothing for us tells us a lot about the kind of people we should want to be anyway.

●················●················●

Even when the whole crew is kicking butt, it's not always going to be roses. As Winston Churchill supposedly said, "Success is going from failure to failure with no loss of enthusiasm." There will be setbacks, but with a high-functioning team, everyone already understands that. However many *no's* it takes to get to a *yes* is how many it's going to take. Nothing gets achieved if you give up on the goal. As such, it's not just about getting to *yes*, it's about surviving *no*.

When we pass judgment, wash our hands of responsibility, shirk our duties, hoard what we know for fear someone will do it better, or expect others to do things the exact same way we would, we not only fail our employers and coworkers but also ourselves. By contrast, when we tackle impediments together, allow our peers to contribute, do our best, and move through difficulties by refocusing on our common aspirations, we function as our greatest selves. That's when things happen, and life's too short not to make things happen.

• •

"Rock 'n' roll singer in a rock 'n' roll band" is the job in my life that has brought me the most satisfaction by a landslide. I know some of you might assume that's a given. I understand where you're coming from, but trust me when I tell you it's a lot of hard work. Throughout this book, I share time and time again tales of humiliation, rejection, and failure. I encourage you to review them if you doubt that what I say is true. Having provided that caveat, I will concede that when it's good—when it's *really* good—it's like floating. It's falling in love. It's orgasm. It's sitting down at a banquet to dine upon a grand rich meal; you may fill up, but you'll always get hungry again. There is a level of cosmic communication between musicians that is possible—elusive, but possible.

In the fall of 2012, I toured the United States with my

band. They had been with me for more than 10 years, and we had sold hundreds of thousands of tickets and records, played all over the world, and done more than perhaps any of us had dreamed possible. We had learned how to function as a highly efficient unit. Like a phalanx wherever we went, we knew how to complement each other. When there were issues, we learned to attack the problem and not the individual. The work wasn't something we had to do, it was something we *got* to do. Whether we were visiting a radio station, stuck in a snow storm, or out socially at a friend's wedding, we all knew our roles, and for an extended moment in time, it was a beautiful thing.

I was the ringleader of this talented circus. There was Boots Factor playing the drums with his Levon Helm–esque shoulder drop and honey-laden vocals. Sam Getz on the pedal steel with a big beard and legendary guitar sound that later led him to reach millions with his own band, Welshly Arms. Kit Karlson, my right-hand man, who would respond to every lyric, sideways glance, and crowd encouragement as though he was born on stage. And Chip Johnson, cool and steady playing the bass like he knew something we all wanted to know. Toward the end of our time together, we would improvise long sections of music as though we had rehearsed them for years. And in a way we had.

WHEN NOTHING WORKS

Great artists don't always make great people. Great leaders don't always make great followers. Ideas that look good on paper sometimes don't pan out. There is just no accounting for taste. And these are only a handful of the reasons things fall apart.

When all attempts to do a job have been exhausted, when we've given up the need to be right in favor of finding resolution, when we've salvaged what's to be salvaged and *still* come up empty, we either move on or we die inside. It's that simple.

Lots of us will cling to professions we don't really want or aren't very good at. We have egos to protect and pride to think about, not to mention fiduciary responsibilities. Choosing between obligations to our family and having our spirit flattened is no joking matter, and sometimes our only satisfaction may be that we've done what needed to be done. But, however daunting the prospect may be, we can't stay stuck in vocations that crush our soul and make us feel wretched for one moment longer than necessary. We mustn't let our fear of finding a new post, one for which we are better suited, stop us from improving our life. It's vital to our well-being that when the situation has grown pernicious, we find a way to leave it.

● ················· ● ················· ●

People ask me if my group the Sixers will reunite. It always feels a bit insensitive to me, like asking a divorcée if they intend to get back together with their ex. It wasn't my idea to split up, but after talking it through with the others, I saw the wisdom in it. Also...it was out of my control. Sometimes we think we know what's best for us when, in fact, we don't. Events occur that cannot be planned for. The market changes, the business closes, someone dies. There is no more surefire way to get stuck than by clinging to the past, trying to deconstruct events that were never ours to command. We might as well try to control the weather.

When it came to my band's dissolution, I may not have chosen that path, but I grew to accept its inevitability. Chopping wood the day after our last performance, I felt sad but also free. When you aren't supposed to be working together anymore, the best thing that can happen is to disembark.

It's been more than seven years since we broke up. Every so often, Shady, who is still a part of my crew, will catch me reminiscing and getting a little verklempt. I'll look at him and ask that he try to pretend I'm acting like a man. He'll remind me that it's been a marvelous seven years. I daresay the best of my life.

SO WHAT HAVE I LEARNED?

I've learned that the best job security is to be great at what you do, and you'll be greater at what you do if the work matters to you. Do a good job and they're not going to want to fire you. Do work you care about and you're not going to want to quit.

I've learned we should always consider the other people in the room no matter how inconsequential their role may seem. We all have to find our own hustle.

I've learned that failure is a given, nobody's perfect, but sometimes a collection of imperfect humans can make magic.

I've learned that when it's time to cut your losses, there's only one way out and it's the high road, so no use looking for another exit.

Mostly, more than anything else, what my coworkers have taught me is the power of humility. We do the best we can with what we've got, and this is true for everyone everywhere who has ever worked a blessed hour.

IRISH GOODBYE

Remember when we got high behind the house?
By the garage so the kids would not find out
The cat's on Prozac and no one seems to care
The party's packed but you feel like no one's there

You were born with everything you need
So wear that heart of yours on both your sleeves

A mother's holding her baby on the plane
The kid is crying, a businessman complains
You hear the whispers and see the eye rolls too
I guess we've all got some growing up to do

You were born with everything you need
So wear that heart of yours on both your sleeves
They'll get the best and the worst of you
There'll be some days that you can't get through, but please
Wear that heart of yours on both your sleeves

You give your heart to someone
Because it's yours to give
And only when they break it
Do you realize what you did
There is a sword that's hanging
Right above all our heads
It is suspended, it is suspended, it is suspended by a spider web

So check your phone every minute for an hour
Irish goodbye, the greatest superpower

You were born with everything you need
So wear that heart of yours on both your sleeves
You have got the best and worst of me

So wear that heart of yours on both your sleeves
Both your sleeves
Both your sleeves
Both your sleeves

CHAPTER 9

A SENSE OF HUMOR

L ife is absurd, tedious, and painful.

I can't imagine a more fitting place to start a chapter about having a sense of humor than by recalling the time I walked out for a performance with toilet paper sticking out of the back of my jeans. I wish this was a fictional anecdote, but much to my chagrin, it isn't. The thing is, just before taking the stage I heard the group of girls behind me say, "Oh my God, does he have toilet paper coming out of his pants?" And I simply refused to acknowledge it. Kind of like the way a dog sticks its head, and nothing else, under the bed in a thunderstorm. Once I arrived on stage and confronted the situation, my humiliation was complete, but what could I do except see the farce in it?

And this is the point I'm about to make repeatedly. When faced with the choice between laughter and tears, laughter is the better alternative. There will be no shortage of tears. But without our sense of humor, we are going to experience trauma with limited recourse.

Time and time again, my sense of humor has saved me. Sometimes it did so in obvious ways, but just as often it was through a subtle shift in perspective that a loss became a win. I can remember one instance where, after months of separation, I arrived in Florence, Italy, to reunite with Kirsten who had been studying abroad. Three male houseguests, who had shown up moments earlier, unannounced, greeted me at the door of her apartment; they were hoping to crash on her couch. I was fit to be tied. I wanted them to leave right away, but Kirsten, being the more hospitable member of our team, insisted we do nothing until the morning. It was tense to say the least. That is until the boys and I found ourselves commiserating about European toilets (which can be a bit lackluster in terms of water pressure and cleaning the actual toilet bowl). I don't remember much else about the Boboli Gardens except that when the guys and I somehow stumbled onto our fear of having to go number two and leave a mess that the girls would see, we ended up laughing until our sides hurt. They stayed the whole week, and honestly, I was sad to see them go.

Our ability to diffuse tension by observing the unintended comedy in life is a blessing, and if we mine the debacles of our past, we can often find joy in them.

I'll go first; but before I do, a word on the intent of humor.

THE INTENT OF HUMOR

I've always loved a good practical joke. I used to spend my birthday money on itching powder and whoopee cushions. If you can get someone to sit on a whoopee cushion without knowing it's there—I still think that's about the funniest thing in the world. And if a person sees it on their seat and sits on it anyway for the benefit of those in attendance, mad respect. One of my favorite things about new friends is that they aren't privy to any of my silly antics yet, nor I to theirs. It's open season.

But there's a difference between being funny and having a sense of humor. They are not the same. Everyone who is funny, by definition, has a sense of humor, but not every-one who has a sense of humor is funny. See the difference? Whether or not you're a humorous person is insignificant to the overall quality of your life, but having the ability to be amused is vital.

My daughter tells me she likes her boyfriend because he makes her laugh, but I've met him, and he's not funny. At least not around me. I can only assume then that they both have a great sense of humor. Now I've said this onstage dozens of times in the months since they started dating. It always gets a big response. But I only feel comfortable making the joke because I like the guy and he knows I like him. If I didn't, it wouldn't be the same. People might still be tickled pink by my comment, but if I weren't a fan, it would just be unkind. This is what happens when we laugh *at* people, instead of *with* people. We may find something hilarious, when in actuality a person's feelings are being hurt, and that's never funny.

Sometimes we try to evoke humor and fail miserably. I once made a show of tossing my friend's hat into the crowd after he botched some lyrics while performing with me. I meant it as a goofy gesture in the face of a would-be embar-rassment. He was balding, though, and quite sensitive to his appearance, and I hadn't considered that it might be upsetting to him to lose his lid in public. He didn't speak to me for almost a year afterward. The problem wasn't his sense of humor, but more that my intentions weren't clear—he thought I was genuinely pissed at him, and in that light, my reaction came across as mean-spirited.

For my part, I've never been put off by a well-placed crack at my own expense, so long as it came from someone I knew and it felt genial in its intent. In college, I never minded when a housemate would pour freezing cold water over the top of the shower curtain or steal my towel. I happen to have a spindly physique that has also been the inspiration for plenty of good-natured ribbing. I'm built kind of like Teen Wolf, gangly and hairy, and the observation of my modest anatomy has been the source of much mirth amongst those who know me well. I'm OK with that. I can laugh at myself. But the motive is critical. Feeling like you're the punch line of someone's ill-intentioned wisecrack just sucks.

Last fall at back-to-school night, I could see in my peripheral vision the guy to my left looking me up and down. He kept glancing back and forth from me to the others seated at our table in what appeared to be an effort to get their attention. When the teacher finished with her presentation, I turned to face him. With a grin that can only be described as insufferable, he unloaded the remark he'd been so eager to share. He watched the faces of the other parents, seeking their approval as he said, "It's a little early for mustache season, isn't it?"

I barely knew this guy, and he was attempting to insult my appearance as we sat in tiny plastic elementary school chairs. *Seriously, Biff, if you don't have anything nice to say, don't say anything at all.* That's what I wished I had said, but instead I just mumbled that it was never a bad time for a mustache.

•·················•·················•

Anytime I'm tempted to tease someone, I try and ask myself first how I feel about that person. If I realize I don't care for them, I keep my mouth shut. It wouldn't be funny. It would be cruel. The one group that, in my opinion, deserves a pass when it comes to poking fun is *professional comedians.*

These spiritual treasures are the uncertified doctors of joy, those who risk their own ego in service of a laugh. Through a trial-and-error process that would discourage even Henry Ford, they manage to produce tiny "bits," illuminating life for the rest of us. As such, I'm inclined to afford them a wider berth than, say, a boss or neighbor. Without a vast aperture, how will they know where the boundaries are? And, even if we do decide to cut them some slack, it's not like we're doing them any real favors here. No one intentionally puts their foot in their mouth as often as a professional comic. A displeased patron once asked Dave Chapelle for her money back during a performance, and in one of my all-time favorite comebacks he responded by saying, "I'm like Evel Knievel, I get paid for the attempt."

So if a sense of humor costs so much and can be perilous to a relationship, why do we bother risking it? Because laughter, aka "the best medicine," boosts the immune system, decreases stress hormones, and triggers the release of endorphins, the chemicals that make our body feel good naturally. Also, life is absurd, tedious, and painful.

LIFE IS ABSURD

Everybody on earth is the result of an orgasm. I mean, how hilarious is that? With lots of cultures hung up on sex as an act of indecency, we pause for a moment to realize that, test tube babies aside, we only exist because two people had sex. Maybe they loved each other, maybe they didn't. Even if they loved each other, maybe they didn't get along well. It doesn't matter. We made it. We're here. But when we consider the deed that got us here? Let the shame begin.

As I already mentioned in the chapter on health, I think sex is wonderful, and I've always been, more or less, comfortable discussing it. When I was 12, my parents signed me up to be on a panel of preteens who went on 107.9 WEBE to share their thoughts on the topic. This was a huge station with a massive reach over most of Connecticut. I'm sure people I knew were listening, but I don't remember feeling self-conscious about any of it. Maybe my mother-in-law could tell this about me. And maybe that's why she decided to call Kirsten and I one evening to talk about the two vibrators she found in her 19-year-old son's sock drawer.

"What should I do?" she inquired. It's an interesting moment in a kid's life when their parents start asking them how to handle situations. We were under the impression that our parents would always be the ones giving the advice, and it's a turn of events the first time they seek our opinion, a bit like Dorothy discovering Oz behind the curtain. You realize that they only know what they know and not much more.

My first reaction when she told us of her discovery was one of pride. I didn't know Sean, the baby of the family, had it in him. I had to chuckle at the thought of my quiet, seemingly innocent, sibling-in-law being a liberated youth. Two years earlier he had visited us at our one-bedroom apartment, where we lived out of wedlock, and he'd asked where Kirsten slept. Now he was stashing not one but two sex toys in his dresser while heading off to college for a couple months. Did he really imagine there was no chance anyone would look in his drawers while he was away?

In the end, we assured Kirsten's mom it was nothing to be concerned about and decided he'd probably be too embarrassed to discuss it. We did what any Irish Catholic family would do; we acted like it didn't happen. The contraband was thrown out, and it wasn't discussed except in hushed tones, and never with my brother-in-law. One night, some months later, I was having beers with Sean when I decided on my old standby—the truth. "So what's with the dildos, bro?"

"What?"

"It's cool man. I don't care about any of that stuff. I think it's great, but why did you leave them at home?"

"What?" he said again, his face blank.

"Seriously man, we *all* know."

"Wait. What?" he seemed genuinely flummoxed.

Thus, began the unraveling of an adventure that involved a unique, and not entirely courteous, houseguest who had stayed over earlier in the year and used my brother-in-law's room. Turns out the tenant had left some parting gifts. Events revealed that Sean had found an altogether different "massager" and disposed of it on the quiet, while the pair of dongs later uncovered by my MIL went undetected by him. Through a substantial amount of sleuthing, we cleared up the mistaken identity, but not really. Once something like that hits the rumor mill, it's hard to take back. He still gets the stink eye from certain extended family members when saying grace for the holidays, as if to say, "Oh, *he's* going to save our souls."

● ⋯⋯⋯⋯⋯⋯ ● ⋯⋯⋯⋯⋯⋯ ●

My big day in the theater of the absurd came a few years later when I got my vasectomy. Let's just say that my urologist greatly undersold the procedure. "You'll be playing tennis within a day or two," he told me with a hearty smile. I had no reason not to believe him and decided to drive myself to the appointment. I was already scheduled for the snip when we had gotten the surprise news that baby number four was on the way, and I wondered if we were the most irresponsible people on the planet.

The operation itself was uneventful. Not how I'd choose to spend a spring vacation, but bearable for sure. It was when I sat up and felt like I had just chugged a quart of whiskey that I started to worry a little. Forced to lie back down, they gave me some OJ and told me the lightheadedness would pass. It did not. Hours later, when it was time for the nurses to go home, I rang Kirsten and asked if she might be able to come pick me up. "I'm sorry, babe, I'm a couple hours away. I thought you didn't need a ride." *Yeah, me too.*

I phoned a number of friends to see if they could bail me out, but no one was answering. I rang the only person guaranteed to take an unexpected evening call from me: my mother. "Mom, can you come get me at the doctor's office? I can't drive and everyone here needs to go home." She was understandably concerned, and I was in over my head yet again, but I had to admit, it was kind of funny.

I'll never forget being 36, sitting there in the waiting room with the receptionist, and telling my mom, "I just got a vasectomy and, oh yeah, we're having another baby." Was I embarrassed? Yeah. Probably kind of like Sean felt when he realized most of his family thought of him as a regular Ron Jeremy for a couple months during his freshman year in college. But when life throws you a curve ball, if you're not laughing, you're crying.

LIFE IS TEDIOUS

Beyond the reach of silliness awaits the dreary realm of tedium. It was one of those 6:20 a.m. flights. You have to be there an hour early, and it can take forever to get through morning traffic in a city like Chicago. The only option is to set your alarm for the middle of the night and cobble together three hours' sleep if you're lucky. Boarding the plane, the guy behind me started whistling the Billy Joel song "Allentown." Now I'm a Billy Joel fan, but that tune, whistled publicly, at that time of day? That's just downright annoying. And in terms of places that us human folk annoy each other, planes rank right up there.

So, when in the summer of 2009 I found myself taking 28 flights in 31 days, I braced for monotony. Our band and crew were on a military tour visiting several countries and spending hours waiting around airports trying to clear security, customs, transportation holding patterns, you name it. It felt as though we'd been hired by the United States Armed Forces to basically sit around airport lounges. The shows themselves were brief, lightly attended, and comically far apart from each other. We came to know well the old saying "hurry up and wait." It wasn't long before we grew listless.

It may have been Lisbon, or possibly Istanbul, but whenever "the clap" first happened, it helped. Sometimes on an international route, everyone applauds when the plane lands. The tradition is usually the result of a very long or very perilous flight. Our gang decided to see how far we could take that custom. At first we stuck to the script, just trying to lead the charge and see what kind of enthusiasm we could glean from our fellow travelers. After a day or two, though, we started pushing the envelope. On short domestic flights, we'd clap. A successful takeoff? We'd clap. Good news from the cockpit? Let's let our flight crew know they're appreciated!

Because we were seated in different parts of the aircraft, it wasn't clear that we were an entourage, and before long the whole plane would erupt with applause. The concept took hold, and all of a sudden, we looked forward to downtime to see where else we could stage similar coups. We'd spread out in the urinal and one of us would start to hum a tune. On cue each of us would chime in until we couldn't keep from busting up. Complete strangers would join us too. Why? Because laughter is contagious. Looking back on that tour, I can't tell you whether the troops enjoyed our music or not, but I can say with certainty that we did some fine diplomatic work for the USA as ambassadors of good humor.

....

On another occasion, the brining of the Thanksgiving turkey was entrusted to Kirsten and me. I'm not sure why. In terms of culinary acumen, we rank quite low compared to other members of our family. Still, we try to do what's asked of us.

With careful precision we added rosemary, sage, and thyme to the "brining bag." Thirty pounds of poultry lay in my hands as I descended the steps to our basement refrigerator, where the bird was to marinate for 24 hours. As I reached to put it on the shelf, the fowl slipped from the plastic bag and fell to the concrete floor of our unfinished basement, where it seemed to roll for an eternity. At first it spiraled along, skittering in the juices of the sizable splash that our special seasoning had made, but eventually it rolled past that circumference and onto the chalky part of the floor.

It's unclear whether or not the three-second rule applies in an instance like this, and we'll never know what that turkey might have tasted like had it not lain there on the ground for the better part of a minute as we doubled over. Much as I didn't relish the responsibilities of preparing the meal, and much as I still have concerns about what unsavory chemicals we may have later ingested, I would no sooner trade the memory of the runaway turkey than cut off an appendage.

More recently I was working a long day in my office when my wife delivered me a panini from our favorite lunch spot. I mentioned that evening that I felt our go-to restaurant might be slipping; the food was really soggy. "There's a few reasons for that..." Kirsten began. Only then did she reveal that an entire glass of water had spilled on my salami and cheese. It gave me flashbacks. I never heard what the other supposed reasons were for my damp midday meal, and I could have opted to be annoyed that she had gone ahead and knowingly served me a wet sandwich, but instead we had a solid chortle about the whole thing.

Does everybody have memories like these they can tap into? Instances when, amidst the daily grind, something happened to break the routine. Perhaps we found them stressful while they were going on. Maybe these were moments when we should have laughed but missed our opportunity to see the humor in the situation. We may not have realized that life is absurd, tedious, and painful, and our ability to laugh at it is sometimes our greatest coping mechanism.

It's not too late. I hope my extended family remembers that when they read about the 2015 turkey. I'm sorry we didn't tell you. I guess we just kind of "forgot." Anyway, you're fine. If you were going to get sick, it would have happened a long time ago. Also, now you know why I favored the stuffing and mashed potatoes that year.

LIFE IS PAINFUL

The last time I saw my father's father, "Grampy" Kellogg, I asked him a simple question. "Anything left on your bucket list?" He was a man of few words and sat there for a minute before he answered.

"Only thing left on my bucket list is to kick it." Sweet Jesus, what a response. I did some research to see who else might have said that before and couldn't find anyone of note. It doesn't matter. When I think of my grandfather, I think of him saying those words and then letting a wry smile creep across his face, lighting up his eyes. I told that story at his funeral. I was pleased to tell it, and my family was pleased to hear it. We were sad, but we were happy.

I've always preferred the two-for-one catharses package of a good laugh *and* a good cry, but not everyone lives as close to the water as I do. For plenty of folks, tears don't come quite so readily, and so humor ends up being their best bet for a little relief from the pain of life. There's no way to sugarcoat it: Life hurts a lot. This, we know.

While I was writing this book, I played a 40th birthday party for Andrea. She had a wife and a 7-year-old. She was dying. She gave me a list of songs to play at her party, and there were a lot of heavy ones on there. I had intended to curate a slightly more ebullient playlist for the guests, but it was apparent that this was likely to be her final birthday, and far be it for me to deny someone's last wishes. I walked on stage, trying to steady my breathing, and looked out at her family and friends. Her dad. Her mom. Her daughter. There was sadness on every single face I set my gaze upon, all except Andrea's.

"Hello, everyone, my name is Stephen Kellogg. Andrea picked the set list, so if you don't like it, blame her." Off we went, big smiles (and some happy tears). The laugh opened up the airways, literally and figuratively, for us to move ahead with an emotionally difficult experience—a person's last concert. She died three weeks later, but I'll never forget what it was like to make her feel good that day.

●┈┈┈┈┈┈┈┈●┈┈┈┈┈┈┈●

When the Buddha said, "Life is suffering," he wasn't kidding. Even the best existence is going to be filled with anguish. Big pain calls for a big sense of humor.

Upon learning that Grandma Jean had dementia, it seemed like only a matter of days before she began to forget things. If you've ever experienced the deterioration of a loved one's mind, you know the heartbreaking gut punch of watching them slip away. "Are you making much money?" she'd ask me. I'd give her a nice detailed explanation of my financial particulars. She'd say, "That's good," and seconds later counter with, "So are you making good money?" It felt like Yiayia in *My Big Fat Greek Wedding*, where they keep finding her on the neighbor's lawn. The stress was palpable as we tried, in vain, to remind her who we were and who she was.

But one summer night in the last year of her life, she asked me to fix her a vodka and tonic. Then she asked again, and again. I had never made the drink before or known her as someone who fancied hard liquor, but I was game to try. As I glanced over at Kirsten, she held back tears but managed a smile. We had been watching helplessly for months as the disease took its toll, and I don't think any one of us felt we were allowed to breathe, no less see the absurdity in what we were up against.

In this one moment, though, Grandma Jean wanted a vodka and tonic, and she wanted it now, dammit. And *this*, for whatever reason, struck me as funny. I began to laugh. Then Kirsten began to laugh. Then Grandma Jean was laughing too.

There was nothing humorous about what was happening, nothing at all, and before you think I'm a terrible person for telling you this story, understand something: We all loved Grandma Jean. We were suffering. But without any respite from our distress, we would be left with only sadness. And that wasn't enough. Not for me anyway. Are we not allowed a guilt-free laugh in the face of our deepest despair?

• ⋯⋯⋯⋯⋯• ⋯⋯⋯⋯•

Why am I telling you all this?

Because it feels good to look back on cringe-worthy moments and share them with you. Because when I consider all of the parts of my life that haven't gone as planned, I realize that my sense of humor has been the invaluable friend I never knew I had. The silent companion who was with me every step of the way, helping me see the lighter side of life's many challenges. And I thought maybe if I showed you some of mine, it might help you with yours. You're going to need it, because life is absurd, tedious, and painful.

PRAYERS

So your life did not work out the way you wanted, join the club
The success the others flaunted killed off your remaining buzz
Nothing like you thought you'd be
Believe me I've been there too
When life brings you to your knees, and you feel like you can't move
Know that this is true

Every unkind thing we say leads to our unhappiness
No one in the world gets by without feeling bad sometimes
I'm not trying to be a jerk
But say your prayers, get off your ass, and get back to work

Those who stand for nothing never win much in the end
Just because you don't offend them, doesn't mean that they're your friends
You thought logic would prevail, that the facts would tell the tale
But from what I've seen they'll wear their blind obedience like a veil
Still this rule never fails

Every unkind thing we say only drives the love away
No one in the world gets by without feeling bad sometimes
I'm not trying to be a jerk
But say your prayers, get off your ass, and get back to work

And there's nothing like a dog fight, where everybody thinks they're right
To remind us that a prayer is not an answer, just a light
Even if you're only getting by, start to wonder why you even try
Say the things you need to say...

But if the words won't come to you
Clear your head and tell the truth
No one in the world gets by without feeling bad sometimes
I'm not trying to be a jerk
But say your prayers, get off your ass, and get back to work

CHAPTER 10
INTEGRITY

The truth is never a bad idea.

Sure, it's gotten me in all kinds of trouble in the past (and still does), but not nearly as much trouble as the avoidance of it has. In the name of honesty, I've said and done things that have pissed people off. I know this, but that doesn't mean I regret it. Too often people mistake shooting straight with being difficult. And that's not to suggest that I have *always* told (or tell) the truth. Nor that I have acted honorably in every circumstance. Both of those assertions would be categorically untrue. I've exercised poor judgment, found myself in moral grey areas, and still fall victim to the casual white lies most of us consider harmless (though

I'm not sure if I agree with that assessment). Part of me feels like if you'll lie about little things, you'll lie about big things, and if you'll lie to others, you'll lie to yourself. But, of course, then there are extenuating circumstances...

Suppose a friend delivers a eulogy. She stumbles over her words and speaks so softly that only the people in the very front row can hear her. After it's over she asks, "Was it alright?" What are you really going to say? *It's a fait accompli.* There's no point in making her feel terrible, and yet my inclination is still to find something real to convey in my response. Maybe it's just, "It was clear that you loved your friend with all your heart."

Before you start imagining too many scenarios where you'd prefer to be lied to—like maybe, "Do these jeans make me look fat?" or "Do you think anyone noticed when I introduced the boss's wife by the wrong name?"—be careful what you wish for. If we get comfortable sanctioning untruth, how can we believe the answers to weightier questions like, "Do you still love me?" or "What are the chances of a full recovery?" Inviting dishonesty so that we can gloss over a painful reality is like eating cotton candy for nutrition; you might feel better for about 10 seconds until the queasiness sets in and you realize you've made a terrible mistake.

I'm reminded of those who still repudiate climate change

and cling to the notion that we can treat the earth like a garbage can without any repercussions. Sure, it would be more convenient to pretend global warming wasn't a thing despite an overwhelming majority of scientists throughout the world who feel otherwise, but why would we do that? Why take the chance?

And it's not only the colossal truths that are important to face; it's *all* truths. Suppose a person with bad breath asks you if they have bad breath and you don't answer them honestly. You're not exactly throwing them a bone. Maybe you don't hurt their feelings and on the surface that seems like an act of compassion, but when you think about it, they came to you from a place of trust, and you fed them to the wolves. Now they'll be going about their day with an embarrassing case of halitosis, wondering why others are acting standoffish toward them. As Warren Wiersbe famously said, "Truth without love is brutality and love without truth is hypocrisy." There's no doubt whatsoever the truth can be upsetting, but it's our best bet because without it we're skateboarding on a rowboat in the middle of the ocean.

The concept of integrity, however, is about more than simply telling the truth. Honesty is the nucleus, but a person can theoretically be honest and still not have integrity. Therein lies the rub.

WHAT IS INTEGRITY?

It's one of those words I find myself looking up from time to time just to be sure I still know what it means. I'm guessing it was on all of our vocab tests in school, but knowing the defi-nition of a unit of language doesn't always mean we under-stand it; sort of like looking at a bowl of fruit in a painting versus tasting the apple itself—it's not quite the same. "The quality of being honest" and "having strong moral princi-ples" is how they define it in Webster's dictionary. I can't help pondering my own peccadilloes when I consider it in those terms.

It's easy to forget about all the things I've never gotten caught for: texting while driving, shoplifting Advil, unde-clared goods hidden from the watchful eye of the customs agent, cash under the table, etc. I don't have to tell you because your mind has already gone to your own crimes and misdemeanors. It's tough to throw stones when you live in a glass house, so most of us just pretend ours is made of steel.

My mom used to sit me down at a very young age and implore me to be a "man of my word." I wasn't sure exactly what she meant, but over time something sunk in and I started to get the picture. If ignorance is bliss, my mother wasn't having any of it, and she was committed to my understanding the value of honor. Integrity is a condition you know when you see it.

It's giving the wallet back with the cash still inside it. It's telling your wife you kissed another woman at a dance club in Rio de Janeiro. Leaving your insurance and contact information on the car you accidentally hit in the supermarket lot. It's taking a pay cut when the money gets tight so that your employees can keep their jobs. Knowing the difference between what a person is *willing* to do and *wanting* to do and choosing to favor the latter, rather than be the sort of character who coerces people into doing things they truly aren't comfortable doing.

It's signing your name when you feel the need to share a controversial opinion online and acknowledging when the opposing side makes a valid point you hadn't thought of. Shaking the other team's hand after a tough loss and saying, "Good game," even though you're still hurting from the defeat. It's calling to say you are running late and refusing to make up a phony excuse for why that is. Integrity isn't about not screwing up, it's about owning it when you do.

I'm sure I never considered truthfulness as a sliding scale, though I believe now that it is. Sometimes we're well aware of not being on the up and up, but there are other occasions when the deceptions are so small and happen so fast that they don't even register as falsehoods. That may be standard human behavior, but it doesn't mean it isn't problematic.

Trust, once broken, can be irreparably damaged. The good news about integrity is that it regenerates. We can reset and try again no matter how many times we make a mess of things.

And, thus, begins a brief chronological history of some of my most notorious indiscretions and how I survived them.

BROKEN INTEGRITY

This has the potential to be a long list, and my intention here isn't to abuse myself by reliving every painful lapse in moral fortitude. But, taken in stride, these are a few of my formative experiences that left a lasting impression. They taught me that one's integrity is automatically tied to one's self-worth. In order to be whole (another definition of integrity), we sometimes have to take a good hard look in the mirror and face something we'd rather not see. *Mirror, mirror on the wall, who is the most ashamed freshman of them all...*

I had only been elected to student government for about three weeks when Father Barry caught me cheating on my Western Civilization test. A number of us had our notes underneath the exam, but class had just started when he walked up to my desk and, without a word, took the papers away. The next 40 minutes were among the longest of my life. I thought of what my parents' reaction would be. They had been so proud in the preceding weeks. What would they think now? I wanted to crawl under a rock and disappear.

Father Barry was a dour man to begin with and seemed to delight in my disgrace. He used to kick our desks if he thought we weren't paying attention, and on this day he was full of good cheer, making wisecracks about how he'd "unearthed corruption" and calling me a cheater in front of my peers. What could I say? He was right.

At the end of that wretched period, I took a mournful walk up to the front of the room and asked him point blank if he was going to have me impeached. He told me to take the test home and fill it out for an F grade. It was an incredibly decent thing of him to do and remains to this day the best F I ever got. I learned from a grouchy Jesuit that a failure will not, in fact, kill you, but abandoning your principles just might. Because of him I never cheated on a test again.

●·················●··················●

Having used my very own brains and wits to graduate high school, we flash forward to the summer of 1994, where our hero, and I use the term loosely, is visiting Laconia, NH, on a camping trip with his sister Amy, brother-in-law Paul, and of course, our heroine, Kirsten.

We spent a lot of time camping that summer because it seemed to be the one place our parents would let us go without supervision. For some reason they preferred us shacking up in the woods under a flimsy canvas to hanging around the house each day. But the devil you don't know isn't necessarily better than the one that you do.

On this particular occasion, we—and by *we* I mean *me*—drank several cans of beer while trying to cook the sorriest hot dogs you've ever seen on the sorriest camping grill you've ever seen. By the time dinner was served, I'd say these little chunks of mystery meat were 80 percent lighter fluid. But we were 17 and having our first real taste of freedom, so I ate with gusto and implored the others to do the same. I got no takers, and when the rain started, I think my brother-in-law Paul was relieved to have an excuse to leave the campsite and go into town. Either that or he overreacted to a little thunder in the distance; it's a horse a piece, but the end result was that we piled into Amy's car in a chaotic rush and neither Kirsten nor myself bothered to leave our booze behind. We weren't driving and Amy wasn't drinking. We figured, what could possibly go wrong?

Upon our arrival downtown, we saw that *Forrest Gump* was playing at the movie theater and decided a film might be a fun way to ride out the storm. I stepped from the car, put my Molson Ice onto the roof, and proceeded to begin relieving myself of excess beer and lighter fluid. Kirsten, following my (awful) example, put her Bartles & Jaymes wine cooler onto the top of the car. That's when I felt a tap on my shoulder.

"You don't piss on Main Street."

I knew it wasn't good, but it wasn't until I did a half turn, midstream, that I realized how *not good* it was. The police officer was a young guy with a southern accent. He spoke slowly, deliberately, and in so doing dragged the whole experience out, which, in turn, made it even scarier.

He asked what we were in town for, and after hearing our answer, told us that *Forrest Gump* was a great movie. I thought for a second he was going to let us go; then he put us both in handcuffs and stuffed us in the back of his cruiser. I always remember a family with little kids walking by at the very moment he was telling me that he had decided to only book me for having an "open container" and not for "lewdness." It was a damn good thing, too, because I later learned "lewdness" can in some instances carry sex-offender status. Can you imagine?

He asked for our age and I lied right to his face: "Eighteen." Kirsten once again threw her lot in with an idiot and followed my lead. It turns out that was the wrong answer. Had we said 17, aka the truth, we would have been written a summons and sent on our merry way. But because I hadn't done enough damage already, we were about to head to the station and be booked as adults. I kept telling Kirsten it would be alright, though there was no reason for her to believe me given the predicament I'd already gotten us into.

The moral of this story isn't that I never peed in public again. I still pull off for a pit stop in traffic, and I dare the police to contradict God's law—when you gotta go, you gotta go. No, the moral of this story is that when you lie, you inevitably make a bad situation worse. And when you find yourself in a bad situation, even one you don't feel is of your own creation, it is 100 percent up to you to navigate your way out of it. Following your integrity's lead is bound to be the quickest route. But I'm getting ahead of myself; I wouldn't fully learn that lesson until much later.

• •

In recalling these tales of broken integrity, they take their place in my memory like tiny backyard hills towered over by Mount Kilimanjaro. Mount Kilimanjaro is not the highest mountain in the world, but it's up there, and while no one's life was on the line in the story I'm about to tell you, it was the only time I ever remember feeling that my code of ethics might be forever shattered. I found myself considering whether everything I'd ever been taught about integrity was meant for someone else.

MY MOUNT KILIMANJARO

Like a lot of folks, we kept a bit of cash around the house. We were saving for a vacation, and the idea of putting it all in the bank made me think we'd spend it on more practical things like, say, bills. So each month we would tuck $250 in a white envelope and put it into our sock drawer, because there's something about a sock drawer that makes it seem like Fort Knox. We had saved $5,000 when our getaway fund was diverted to pay blackmail. It was a shakedown a whole lot of people knew about, but nobody seemed to be able to do a damn thing to stop.

• · · · · · · · · · · · · · · · · • · · · · · · · · · · · · · · · · •

In the summer of 2010, I flew to Los Angeles to write a hit song. This is where all hit songs come from, or so I was led to believe. A few months earlier, I had met with my record company. I knew and liked every person in the office, so I took it seriously when the top brass said to me, "Stephen, we're fans. We want you to win, but we need something we can get on the radio. If you'd consider using less-specific dates and names in a few of your songs, we think you could reach a wider audience."

They had a point. I tend to be autobiographical in my writing. Our most recent release at the time was named after my tour manager and, therefore, called "Shady Esperanto and the Young Hearts." Although it had gone to #17 on the Triple A radio charts and was being used by a bunch of TV shows, *Billboard* magazine referred to it as the "worst name for a single" they had ever heard.

The idea was that we would procure a first-rate producer and focus on releasing music that was not only good to listen to but also easy to market. We started with a process of elimination. I shot high. I wrote to Bon Jovi and Sheryl Crow among others. We expected that most of these scenarios might not work out, especially given our relatively modest budget, but of the first 20 producers we approached, only one responded. We were starting to feel desperate, and desperation is the devil's playground.

• • • • • • • • • • • • • • • • • • •

A big part of being signed to a record company, or being a part of any team for that matter, is keeping the air in the balloon. Maintaining enthusiasm is an aspect of the artists' job. But although bullshit sounds fantastically reasonable to the bullshitter, at some point, reality always sets in. When it became clear that we weren't going to land a household name to produce my seventh studio album, the label suggested a guy whom we will call Tom Fuller. Tom had enjoyed success with a couple hits for other artists, and they thought he was a bit of a wunderkind. My gut told me he wasn't for me, but when we spoke on the phone, he did seem to have it all figured out. I should have listened to my gut.

Tom talked about the inevitability of my commercial success and where I had gone wrong in the past, as if it were a simple science experiment. He laughed at my jokes and acted as though the references I brought up were his favorite artists too. There is a lot I don't know in this world, but I'd bet my house on the fact that he never listened to a single song by Bob Seger, despite assuring me that he, too, "loved the *Against The Wind* album." Toward the end of our conversation, he said he was absolutely certain our budget would be no problem at all. He had answered all my questions correctly, and even though somewhere in the back of my mind a voice was screaming at me to hold my horses, he was undoubtedly the path of least resistance, so I hired him on the spot.

•••••••••••••••••••••••••••

Arriving in Los Angeles to begin writing, I left my family amidst the final week of summer break and checked in to a Ramada Inn on the edge of Koreatown. My phone rang, and it was Tom's manager calling to tell me he wouldn't actually be able to start work for a couple days. Let me repeat. I had left my happy home in Connecticut during the precious final days of summer to fly across the country so that I could stay by myself in an overpriced Ramada Inn and wait for Tom to figure out his schedule. It was a foreboding start to say the least.

In essence, the writing process itself wasn't terrible. I would pen the lyrics and he would come up with the music. Tom had embraced the dubious, but somewhat common, industry practice of using songs that were already hits as a guidepost for our future *hit*. Intentionally aping someone else's work still sounds pretty scuzzy to me, but these days we seem to have a higher tolerance for it than ever. It's hardly news when we read about major stars having success with somebody else's music and melodies—the money changes hands and life continues. Ten years ago, though, I had never met anyone who was as shameless in "borrowing" other people's ideas. And Tom appeared to have absolutely no scruples about what was going on, so I fell in line. After all, what did I know? He had hits, I didn't.

●·················●·················●

From the moment our collaboration began, a policy of appeasement went into effect. I could regale you with all of Tom's demands, but I won't. It's no longer important. To hear his side of the story, we expected "champagne at beer prices" and he was simply renegotiating. I think it was more Machiavellian than that, but my point here is not to air dirty laundry. I'm sharing this with you to demonstrate how catastrophic it is to the soul when we ignore warning signs that our integrity is collapsing. And while Tom Fuller's integrity was garbage, so was mine. I had ignored countless indicators telling me I was on the wrong track, and I was about to pay the price for my neglect.

•················•················•

One day that spring, after we had finished about 80 percent of the record, Tom stopped returning my calls. The album wasn't done yet, and the only hard drives containing the last several months' work happened to be in his possession. Amidst no small amount of confusion, we had to reach out to our label and tell them we didn't know where our producer—or our record—was. They had invested $50,000 for us to make an album that we could no longer even locate. That's when the lawyer called, and the sock drawer came into play.

Fuller's attorney gave us two options: Either we come up with an additional $5,000, after which the hard drives would be returned to us and we could finish the album by ourselves, at our own expense, or we could sue Tom and incur limitless legal fees. We turned to our record company and, although sympathetic, they made clear this was our bed to lie in. And lie in it we did.

Indignantly, I paid the bribe with the vacation funds and patched together the remainder of our record. The band broke up less than a year later.

But this isn't a story about Tom Fuller's integrity, or lack thereof, this one's about me. And what I've managed to gloss over in all this is that the album we were about to release, the one with my name on it, had a first single that was a complete fucking rip-off.

● ·················· ● ·················· ●

No one ever said outright that the song sounded pinched. That is until it hit the internet. The tune, that Tom and I had written together, was generally well received by the industry. As a welcomed follow-up to our last mini-success, it started to get some play on the radio almost immediately. Doors that had long been closed were ajar, and at first, the band and I were too excited to consider the odd negative comment that would come in. Then it began in earnest. Videos on YouTube comparing our song to the Simon and Garfunkel classic we had referenced, going back and forth between the two numbers and pointing out the similarities. That's when I did something I should have done back in Koreatown. I listened closely to the song we were accused of taking from. It was supposed to be a "tip of the hat," but far beyond a nod, we had basically copied someone else's homework. As I sat in my office, the evening sun fading outside my window, my 5-year-old daughter came in. "What song is this?" she asked with heartbreaking innocence.

"Paul Simon's song," I answered.

"Daddy, Paul Simon's song sounds like *your* song."

●················●················●

I did not sleep that night. I lay awake and prayed for a solution to my woes. I couldn't speak directly to anyone about it because I was mortified. A lifetime of songwriting and this was to be my scarlet letter. It was the lowest professional moment of my life. My integrity was pulverized.

INTEGRITY REPAIRED

Those of us who have seen the movie *Jerry McGuire* may be able to picture what happened next. I was almost gleeful in blowing the whole thing up. I don't want to aggrandize it in any way. I had been involved in a plagiarism, and I am not the hero of this story. I am just a man who found his way out of a hole.

First, I told my team of my intentions to withdraw the single and write a letter to those who had heard it, saying that their criticism had foundation and the song would be re-written to address that. I then had to break it to the many people who had been working to get it on the radio that I didn't want it played on the radio. I explained that the new version of the song would be much better and wholly original. They explained that radio is a volatile medium that probably wouldn't play me anymore if I insisted on this course of action. We were both right. Fans loved the new rendition of the song, and with a few small exceptions, no radio station has played my music regularly since 2011.

After we dealt with that, I reached out to each member of the label and described to the best of my ability what had happened. I swallowed hard and accepted responsibility for the debacle.

I was sorry. I'm sure no one doubted that. Still, I had put people I liked a lot in a difficult situation. When my manager called to say they weren't renewing their contract with me a few months later, I don't think either of us was surprised. Through it all, Tom Fuller continued to work on other projects and seemed to get a pass for the whole affair. Because it hurt too much to hate him, after a few months I decided to forgive him (more on that little magic trick in the chapter about forgiveness). In a matter of months, my band of 10 years had unraveled, I'd lost my entire administrative team, and my failure was complete. So much for not embarrassing myself.

●⋯⋯⋯⋯⋯●⋯⋯⋯⋯⋯●

But redemption begins with a single step, and that's easy to forget when we're overwhelmed. The moment I faced the music—pun intended—and sought to make it right, I was clean again. The second I stopped fighting that pit in my stomach and acknowledged the error in judgment, my wholeness was restored. People could hate me or not respect me, but they couldn't get to my peace of mind after I made a decision to *try*. Clumsy, faulty, ugly, damage control. Nothing ever works the same after it, but often, it *can* work again.

I sometimes think about who is out there feeling they've done a thing so appalling that they'll never recover from the humiliation. I'd like to give those human beings some encouragement. The average person makes 35,000 decisions a day; we can't be expected to nail them all. This is not about avoiding mistakes but rather addressing them head-on when they do occur. When we trust the instincts that warn us that we're headed in the wrong direction, we honor our moral compass and, in so doing, protect our souls. Like Jiminy Cricket, our integrity is upheld one small voice at a time.

A few years ago, I played a Simon & Garfunkel tribute show in Central Park where Paul Simon came up and shook my hand. He told me I had done a good job. *The New York Times* also gave my performance a glowing review. I slept easy that night.

THE INTEGRITY TEST

I'm going to leave you on a lighter note.

There's a little game we used to play on tour whereby we'd ask each other, "How much money would it take to get you to do _____ (fill in the blank)?" The fill-in-the-blank was always outrageous and often crude. It might involve letting a horse urinate on you or giving an aging rock star a hand job or repeating the consumption of a giant meal you had just finished eating. It was a silly way to stay entertained on long trips, but it also made us think about what our standards were. What was the threshold for abandoning them? It was hilarious to watch how quickly they could fall when faced with the prospect of the almighty dollar. Someone might start out by saying that it would cost a million bucks to consider tattooing their high school gym teacher's face on their back, but upon further evaluation and offers of "tax-free cash," that same person might be in for a few grand.

It's easy to declare one's principles under the cover of darkness, but when push comes to shove, what will we stand for?

My own life has been a journey with moments of both high and low integrity. I like to think the low ebbs have taught me as much as the high ones have, but I know that there will be more of both. How could there not? In my most contemplative moments, when I say my prayers, I pray not for an easy life but for the strength to meet the one I have been given, the will to do what is right and to keep trying when I fail to meet that test. When I'm lost or can't figure out which way to go, I go back to the veracity of what I'm facing. After all, the truth is never a bad idea.

HIGH HIGHS, LOW LOWS

The one making the decision always ends up second-guessed
By a person less decisive who believes that they know best
I wouldn't change a thing, I would make the call again
Shame on you, you could have been a friend

Now it's hard to hear the measure that was with me all the time
Like it was in the beginning, but the past is hard to find
Do you think we'll ever feel the way we felt when we began?
Do you think we'll ever feel that way again?

High highs, low lows
Only one way that the river flows
Was it comedy or tragedy?
Both I would suppose
High highs and low lows

Or that time in Arizona when we laughed until we cried
All the sleepers in the van one by one turned on their lights
And I never hear the Beach Boys without thinking about that song
What a miracle to feel like you belong

Those were high highs and low lows
Only one way that the river flows
Was it comedy or tragedy?
Where did the good times go?
High highs and low lows
To those high highs and low lows

Now when I received your letter, I hung my head and cried
I looked right into the mirror and the mirror doesn't lie
I wrote twenty songs in Nashville, twenty in LA
Twenty for those brothers that I lost along the way
But for every song I wrote, through every single note

I knew I was writing songs just to give myself some hope
I've scattered tiny rocks all across an asphalt road
For some reason I just needed you to know

About these high highs and low lows
Only one way that the river flows
Was it comedy or tragedy?
Where does the money go?
High highs and low lows
To those high highs and low lows

If what you said about me, if I believed that it were true
I'd throw myself upon the mercy of the ocean blue
But most of your critique doesn't sound that much like me
Though I wonder if it sounds a bit like you?

High highs, low lows
Only one way that the river flows
Was it comedy or tragedy?
Who really knows?
High highs and low lows
I've had high highs and low lows
To those high highs and low lows

CHAPTER 11
FORGIVENESS

REASONS TO SEEK FORGIVENESS

1. I acted badly. I can see that now.
2. I was unkind. I said things I never should have said.
3. You were counting on me and I blew it.
4. I have no idea what I need to be forgiven for, but I know that I do.

Whatever the reason, we all need to be forgiven.

ANGER

f you came here to be angry and right, I'm not sure I can help you. That's not how this one goes. Though my years as a songwriter have left me well versed in the art of cultivating an open heart, I'm still mad at several of the people I've had to forgive. It's great to let a person off the hook, but that doesn't mean I'm obligated to like them. And that *doesn't* mean I'm not still carrying some of the bitterness that accompanies being angry. It's like spitting out food you dislike, the taste remains in your mouth.

You see, I was born with an extensive palette of readily available emotions. The passions that make exuberance and empathy easily accessible for me also leave open the door to less desirable feelings like jealousy and resentment. These are the kind of mental states that can make a person physically ill if they're allowed to run wild. With the good comes the bad, I guess, though I'm not sure any emotion is inherently bad. After all, you feel what you feel. If we don't experience our moods in earnest, they basically leak out of our pores anyway. Repressed feelings are like a passive-aggressive yoga teacher, incongruent and not all that useful.

But of all the various states of mind that I encounter, anger is the one for me that never fully goes away. And let me tell you, it weighs a lot. It's hard to admit it, but each day little movies play in my mind of people whom I'm upset with or I imagine as having done me dirty. Mean kids from my salad days, businessmen who screwed me out of money, friends who betrayed my trust, obnoxious customer-service representatives, terrorists, anyone who says anything negative about my children, pet owners who don't bother to train their gigantic scary dogs, and the list goes on from there. These people aren't seeking my forgiveness, but they have it anyway, and whether they know it or not, they're better for it and so am I. Without it, they'd be the subject of bad vibes, and I would be making myself sick.

We all have people in our lives that we are justified in disliking. We may try to suck others into the long-drawn-out details of why we're right and our enemies are wrong. I have a cousin, for instance, who, given the chance, will talk for 20 minutes straight about human beings you do not know but are supposed to work yourself up into a lather over. This is a guy not at all above telling a person he's never met that they have a booger in their nose, so it's not hard to see how he gets into scrapes, but to him they're all newsworthy events. The story's punch line is usually something to the effect of "and I told the guy, I'm not going pay it unless you fix the gutters!" I don't even bother trying to follow along anymore; I just make sure I have enough food and drink to weather the soliloquy.

On plenty of occasions it may be rational to loathe our nemeses. Still, forgiveness is the mandate. It's the only way we preserve our mental and physical health. It sucks, but what are we gonna do? Hold a grudge? As Anne Lamott once said, that's "like drinking rat poison and then waiting for the rat to die." It doesn't work. Let me tell you about the first time I got the 400-pound gorilla of condemnation off my back.

UNDERSTANDING FORGIVENESS

I wanted to go to my high school reunion just to see that the monsters weren't real. So many of the demons that have followed me around over the years came into my life during that period. As such, I've had to learn to forgive a lot of people I no longer know and some I never really knew anyway.

It was the last weekend of summer, and we were all getting our driver's licenses one by one. This was back when there was no waiting period. You would wake up in the morning unable to legally drive a car and with virtually no road experience. By evening you were Steve McQueen, footloose and fancy-free, with as many road rights to go wherever you pleased as someone who had been driving their entire life. All you had to do was putter around the block and pass your 16-question test, at which point you could jam your vehicle full of fellow adolescents, roll the windows down, and crank the music up as you cruised off into the night. For a parent, it must have been terrifying, but as a teenager, it was electrifying.

The freedom was great, but the truth is, we had nowhere to go, so we drove around to different parking lots where we would decide that it was lame either because no one was there or because too many people were there. It was the routine. We might score some fast food or even beers if we had a designated driver, but so long as we didn't have to go anywhere there were adults, we were happy.

One particular evening in the season of newly found independence, we occupied an abandoned lot where I was entertaining my friends, as I often did, with a bit of corny banter. When I get excited, I do this involuntary thing where I stiffen my pointer finger, contort my hand into an almost claw-like position, and talk to it. You read that correctly. I talk to my finger. I also roll my Rs and make a mourning dove–like sound while I do this. Picture Renfield from

Dracula and you kind of get the gist. I don't know where it came from, and I've never met anyone else with this particular tic, but for as long as I can remember, it has always been a habit of mine. In most cases, I'm not even aware I'm doing it unless someone points it out.

It was that kind of story, and I was really enjoying myself when a kid with spiky hair hopped out of his red Jeep Wrangler and approached our group. He came up fast and spoke to me with an urgency that I later came to recognize as aggression, "I heard you were giving dirty looks to Ralph."

In the middle of asking the question anyone in my position would have asked, "Who is Ralph?" he sucker punched me. I saw stars and hit the deck hard. A total potshot, it happened so fast that my face was pressed to the pavement by the sheer velocity of the blow. Had I known what was coming and had an opportunity to train for two years with Mr. Miyagi, I still wouldn't have been able to fight this guy, but that didn't stop him from putting his fist on my face like a boot crunching down on an ant.

I don't blame my friends for not jumping on my assailant. The dude was athletic and clearly game to throw down. Our crew was an odd mix of puny and chunky. More important, we weren't really that type of guys—fighters. No one wanted to be the next recipient of Mr. Cheap Shot's meaty mitts.

Looking back, I think that if I had been born with a stronger build (or muscles of any kind), I would have gotten into more physical fights. I have wild blood. It turns out God has a sense of humor, though, and I've had the same body—one akin to Jughead from *Archie Comics*—since I was 12 years old. No amount of weightlifting has ever affected my lanky frame, so somewhere along the way I was happy to give up the practice. Instead I've had to rely on words and see if there was any truth to the notion that they are mightier than the sword. They sure as hell weren't that night.

Upon his invitation to "settle this once and for all," my voice came out in a high whine, "I'm not going to fight you, you'll kick my ass." It was actually a sensible thing to say and a complete matter of fact, but in the moment, it just made me feel like more of a loser.

By the time I got back on my feet, I could not see out of my left eye. It was completely swollen over and bleeding in the corner. I'm guessing I wasn't the first person that spiky-haired-red-Jeep-kid had punched because he landed the thing like a freaking boxer. I climbed into my friend's 10-year-old blue Saab and put on Alice in Chains' *Dirt* album as we slunk away in full view of the crowd of spectators that had now gathered to watch us retreat. Their faces bore a mix of surprise and vague amusement as we rolled past, and I felt a sense of shame wash over me. Upon finding out, sometime later, that he had picked me out of the crowd at random by asking, "Who is that guy?" it did little to dispel my sense that I was somehow at fault for the attack.

When college finally rescued me from high school and music finally rescued me from college, the incident faded even further from my consciousness. Every so often I'd hear something in the wind about the kid—that he'd gotten hooked on drugs or had a run-in with the law. I think it ultimately went bad for him. That struck me as poetic justice, though it gave me no pleasure.

One day I found myself at a seminar in New York City. I was studying "team building," thinking it could be good for my new band, and we were asked to do an exercise where we had to recall a formative event from our teenage years. Much to my disappointment, my mind kept wandering to spiky-haired-red-Jeep-guy. His presence back in my brain, after the passage of so much time, was entirely unwelcome, but there he was, nonetheless. It's a difficult irony that when we don't want to think about something, it becomes all we can think about. I tried to associate with anything else. The more I angled to get away from it, though, the more I realized I had been bringing him with me everywhere I went. I hadn't forgiven him, and therefore I couldn't possibly get over him.

He was there with me each night when I would get on stage to perform and assume that someone in the crowd wanted to beat me up. If I didn't win them over, they were going to want to fight me. Guys would come up to shake my hand after shows, and I would figure they were going to sucker punch me. I'm not kidding. Enemies until proven otherwise. Here we were on a major record label, playing to thousands of enthusiastic fans every week, but all I saw were potential foes.

Figuring I had very little to lose, what with forgiveness costing nothing, my hope was that I might free myself from the lasting effects of this boyhood memory. And so it came to pass that I stared into a hotel bathroom mirror and intentionally forgave the young man who had punched me in the face all those years ago. I did so without condition, and the result was instantaneous. I experienced a flood of relief as powerful in its immediacy as its calm. It was then that I made a commitment to forgiveness.

I don't know where spiky-haired-red-Jeep-kid is now, or if he's even still alive, but I do know that he must have had some rough stuff going on in his life to have been that violent at such a young age. I've long since chosen to climb out of the cage I shared with him, but in a way I owe him for helping me understand the power of forgiveness. After that day in New York City, I assumed I had it down. Little did I know that the hardest person to forgive is usually oneself.

SEEKING FORGIVENESS

As frustrating as it is to have someone tell you they forgive you when you don't feel you've done anything wrong, it's far worse to seek absolution and be denied it. No one wants to be patronized and acquitted for crimes they did not commit, but neither do we expect to be repeatedly abused once we've shown remorse for our mistakes.

I once scolded my daughter Adeline for breaking a ceramic water fountain, insisting that she had touched it after being told not to. I'm quite sure my dressing down convinced her that she had busted it, as she tearfully apologized and was, I felt magnanimously, forgiven by me. This was all well and good until we discovered two days later that the fountain had bum wiring inside it and had, in fact, broken with no assistance from our wrongly accused offspring. I still feel lousy about it.

The reality for the accuser in all cases is that—accurate or not—the infraction warrants their pardon. My advice is, when an outstretched hand is being offered, we should take it. It requires energy to give someone a break, but it takes way more stamina to stay mad. Why choose war when the possibility for peace exists? Why perpetuate animosity? And when others won't forgive us? That's when we do it for them.

● ⋯⋯⋯⋯⋯⋯ ● ⋯⋯⋯⋯⋯⋯ ●

I fell out with a couple guys a few years back. We'll call them Bo and Derek. I had to make a decision that involved business, and they took it personally. It happens. Overnight, years of close friendship dissolved. It was heartbreaking. Initially I defended myself in letters against what seemed like unfounded barbs at my character. They had insisted that no personal or phone contact was to be had and most of the time didn't bother writing back. Smart. After all, it's impossible to give up the position of righteousness if you don't actually have to engage in a conversation. You see the no-reply tactic practiced in many a grudge match, and while it's effective at holding on to one's belief in one's own correctness, it always strikes me as cowardly and a little bit cruel. I suppose they also knew that, given my strong bent toward communication, this would hurt me the most. In that regard, they were 100 percent accurate.

All efforts to bolster my own position of being on the

high ground were failing to make me feel better. Those in my inner circle would ask, "Why do you care so much?" and I'd think to myself, *Why don't you care more?* Bo and Derek dogged my dreams at night, and for one whole year I read Teddy Roosevelt's sage advice every morning, "It's not the critic who counts; not the man who points out how the strong man stumbles or the doer of deeds could have done them better. The credit belongs to the man who is actually in the arena." I believed it, but I still felt crappy.

Over time, though, I began to evaluate my own role in the rift. Even if their angst struck me as misplaced, it was real. It didn't come out of nowhere, and I had been the cause of it. I had hurt them whether I intended to or not. When you hurt someone, the appropriate response is to apologize, so that's what I did. Though I wasn't sure of all the details of what I had done to upset my friends to this degree, I had to admit that when I traveled our mutual history, I found plenty of things for which I could have said, "I'm sorry." Is it really that hard to take responsibility for the ways in which we damage each other?

I had been worried that seeking forgiveness would make me seem weak, or worse, guilty. Instead, when faced with my own imperfections, I realized they were just that, lapses in awareness. Times when I was blind to the man I should have been. Who I was wasn't likely to change anytime soon. But shifting one's perspective is not a weakness, it's a willingness to evolve. We can grow, if only by degrees. How many times have college kids prayed to the porcelain god after a night of too much booze only to find themselves there again the following weekend? Eventually, though, with a bit of grace, they get past it. It's a humbling thing to crave clemency. Humbling, but not diminishing. We can be good without being perfect. And we can forgive our own frailty because we're all broken in some way.

There is a Hebrew custom where once you've asked wholeheartedly and been denied forgiveness three times, it becomes the other person's problem. If they pass on their chance at being big by opting to stay small, then it's on them. I wish I could offer you a more storybook ending on this one, but I can't. What I can say is that we will never have accord so long as we attach ourselves to an end result beyond our control. I had to not only give the guys a pass for the hurt they caused me, but also myself for the hurt I had caused them. If they weren't up for taking my olive branch, then I had to lay it down gently at their doorstep and know that I had done my best. I had to forgive myself for letting something I loved slip away. Only then did my dreams become my own again.

PRACTICING FORGIVENESS

Forgiveness is ongoing. It's not a one and done. A runner is a runner because they continue to run. If they stop lacing up their shoes and hitting the treadmill, then they were a runner once upon a time, but they aren't anymore. And so it is with the messy process of forgiveness. Just because we do it once, doesn't mean we're experts. And just because we've granted it in the past, doesn't mean we're going to experience the serenity that comes from practicing it on a daily basis. It needs active maintenance. It's a verb that only looks like a noun. Forgiveness is open-ended, something we have to wake up every day and do again. Especially when we find ourselves reliving the worst of what life can throw at us.

I have a close friend whose parents were murdered at the point of a gun. I cannot imagine there is day that passes where he doesn't think of what was taken from him. And yet, in one of the most gracious acts I have ever known, he wrote to the killer in jail and forgave him. No one would have blamed him if he hadn't, but I suppose he grew tired of carrying the burden. Given the situation, it's hard to conceive of getting to that place for even a single day, no less in perpetuity, but to hear him explain his decision, it was "the best available option."

I struggle to comprehend mercy on that scale. I wrestle with whether or not absolution is mine to give when I think about a tragedy like Sandy Hook. That day of infamy happened so close to where I live, so close to my heart, that it fills me with rage when I recall the sick young man who robbed so many of their joy. I can remember like it was yesterday, calling my mother and telling her that I didn't know where to direct my anger. "But you know exactly where to direct your love," was her response. My fury did nothing for the living. It couldn't bring back the deceased, and it was incapable of healing anything or anyone. Forgiveness, though, is the root of love. And love might be the only emotion that keeps us going in a world where something as heinous as Sandy Hook is allowed to happen. And that's worth considering.

If my friend can show monumental kindness in the face of unspeakable loss, surely we can absolve those who have wronged us in much lesser ways? Surely we can...right?

I'm afraid not.

We rant and rage against each other as though we're the only ones who make any sense. I believe it's because we mistakenly associate forgiveness with condoning the behavior that hurt us in the first place. But that's never been what it's about. It's about choosing to move past the pain. It's about greeting the old ghosts you thought you'd dealt with ages ago and excusing them anew for whatever they did. It's about hearing your internal critic rip you to shreds and call you names and then responding by saying, "It's OK. I still love you."

I have done many things of which I am not proud. I have lied. I have spoken harshly to those I love the most. I have failed to be on time to important events, raised my voice to my grandmother, and made promises I couldn't keep. I've done all this and worse. As far as I know, I have been forgiven. How wonderful.

I have been too humble and too arrogant. I forgive myself.

I have been stolen from, cheated on, disrespected to my face and behind my back. I have been used, underappreciated, and, in a few instances, come to physical harm because of others. As a citizen of the world, I have watched as awful actions played out from the bottom-feeders of society. I forgive them all. Not because I'm a particularly good person, but because vengeance, criticism, and cruelty are an albatross around our necks. By wishing kindness on our enemies, we remove the friction. It's why humility is so attractive. It doesn't force itself but, rather, acts as a balm to the sting.

Those who most needed my forgiveness probably never asked for it, but I'm proud of the fact that I've never withheld it. It's a commitment that I make because I'm not up to the task of holding a grudge. Honestly, neither are you.

SYMPHONY OF JOY

If I don't leave a bank account or plans how to proceed
If I don't give you what you want, I hope you get the things you need
Give my brother the guitars, tell my sister sorry I lost touch
Tell my mama not to worry about money quite so much

Never turn your back upon a second chance
Never trust a guy who says he doesn't...I know you need to...

Dance, like a symphony of joy
And it's not your obligation to go easy on the boys
'Cause the ceiling's gonna shatter and believe me when it does
Those who pinned you to the margins, baby they'll be sweeping up

It ain't nobody's station to tell others how to live
But we've got a situation here where evil still exists
You can't turn away, you've gotta have a dog in every fight
When you see one going rogue don't back down just 'cause he bites
That's right, that's life

You should drive 'em wild every time you get the chance
You've got choices that I'm just not sure you know you have...you gotta

Dance, like a symphony of joy
And it's not your obligation to go easy on the boys
'Cause the ceiling's gonna shatter and believe me when it does
Those who pinned you to the margins, baby they'll be sweeping up

Never turn your back upon a second chance
Never trust a guy who says he doesn't...
Everyone needs to, everyone needs to, everyone needs to...

Dance, like a symphony of joy
And it's not your obligation to go easy on the boys

'Cause the ceiling's gonna shatter and believe me when it does
Those who pinned you to the margins, baby they'll be sweeping up
Dance, like a symphony, a symphony, a symphony...
Baby, you've got the joy

CHAPTER 12

LEGACY

I told you in the introduction of this book that *you* matter. Now I'm going to tell you that your legacy is the reason why. You'll be leaving one behind, whether you intend to or not, so you might as well be intentional about it. That doesn't mean it won't all go to shit, but at least you'll have made an effort, and that's gotta be worth something.

WHY LEGACY?

Late at night, when life's busy gallop slows to a trot, I find myself alone with my thoughts, and sometimes it's terrifying. My anxiety and frustration have a tendency to rise to the surface and demand attention when things get quiet. I think about dying. I think about not really living. I consider what it will be like when everyone who once knew me is gone. Where does that leave my ever having existed? I agonize over world leaders who have no business being world leaders and social issues that tear at the seams of our shared humanity. I fixate on people in my life who aren't doing what I want them to do. I replay past failures and fret about those that lie ahead. I worry for myself, but even more for my loved ones. My brain overflows with what has happened, is happening, or could happen to them. As Thomas Harris once wrote, fear is "the price of an imagination."

And it's not just the big stuff that concerns me. It's the little things too: the cost of a visit to the vet, the disappearance of checkout clerks at the grocery store, people that drive too fast in residential neighborhoods, or, worst of all, those misguided souls who are under the impression that it's OK to talk while someone is performing—they're all on my list. My wife calls me Minor Injustice Man because I'm capable of genuine indignation over seemingly small inequities.

If it sounds a bit depressing, it sometimes is. No wonder I'm keen to stuff 10 pounds of shit into a five-pound bag. It keeps me occupied. Distracted. Being a workaholic and living on the edge of what I'm capable of accomplishing on any given day prevents me from having to confront everything I haven't done yet. Existential queries like, "Is this what I'm meant to be doing?" and "What does it all really mean?" are kept at bay by a busy schedule. The problem with all this avoidance is that, in ducking the issues that come up when we're scared or stressed, we deprive ourselves of the chance to find answers to really important questions.

Mary Oliver asks of us, "What is it you plan to do with your one wild and precious life?" It's a straightforward ask that's really more of a directive, designed to get our juices flowing. Our aspirations may not all come to fruition, but when we attempt to answer her question, we take the first step in building a legacy. And I'm not saying it's easy or that we shouldn't find the prospect intimidating. It's nerve-wracking to consider that everything we do is being cosmically recorded into the DNA of history. But anxiety, if we allow ourselves to see it this way, is valuable information. It's the brain's way of telling our body that there is something we need to address. And when we embrace, rather than attempt to bury, the uneasy feelings that accompany our life choices, we receive the wakeup call that there are meaningful decisions to be made every single day.

By indulging our philosophical preoccupations, we're

less apt to feel like grunts aimlessly grinding out a daily to-do list. Legacy is what gives us purpose. It's a chance to have our presence mean something to someone. Think how different a day could feel if we knew we were affecting the course of another person's life over the next 24 hours. Wouldn't that awareness have a dramatic impact on the way we get out of bed in the morning?

A unique journey all our own with no prerequisites—it's the opportunity to have a say in that for which we will be remembered. This attempt to make your life matter is what I call *the intended legacy*.

THE INTENDED LEGACY

Most of us will not make the history books. A few may have some distant connection to historical significance—Steve Jobs's first employer, a cousin of Rutherford B. Hayes, or Barbra Streisand's dad maybe. But even with the advent of Google, it's unlikely we will be remembered by the wide world. As I see it, there are two ways to feel about that. The first is to be flattened by it. The second is to take comfort in our own tininess.

Understanding that we are an infinitesimal part of the universe puts things in perspective. The stupid remarks or small errors in judgment that feel cataclysmic to us in the moment should hardly matter when we consider that the Earth has existed for 4.5 billion years and our average life span is only 79 of them. Like bugs, we are operating on a limited scale. The strongest ant in the colony may be able to carry a thousand times its body weight, but that's still only a fraction of an ounce. So why take ourselves so seriously if even the people with the greatest accomplishments go the way of the dodo? Because it's all we really have—caring, that is.

In the context of any one person's life, the little things mean almost as much as the big things, and without contradicting what I just said about *unintentional* mistakes, I've observed in my life that *intention* goes a long way. This is good news for those of us seeking purpose. It means that the way we raise our children counts for something. That a mediocre athlete like me gets to show up as Coach Kellogg and teach seventh-grade girls what I know about team spirit. That our random acts of kindness are not merely drops in the ocean. That serving the best coffee in Franklin County for 20 years is an achievement to be celebrated. It means that even if we've done lots of things wrong, we can begin a process of redemption by making right choices. We can seek to improve our legacies.

•·················•·················•

What is it you would like to be remembered for? Let that marinate. It's the kind of question we must answer for ourselves. Our parents, teachers, and bosses, try as they might, do not get to fill in this particular blank. It's ours and ours alone to decide. I suggest thinking about it right now.

Here is my answer: I've had a love of words and a compulsion to write them down for as long as I can remember. Phrases occur to me and I turn them into song lyrics, essays, internet posts—you name it. I view these collected thoughts as a document of my best intentions, the intellectual articulation of my heart. It never matters to me what format they end up in just so long as I've recorded the point of view. Journals, notebooks, and scraps of paper line the shelves in my office.

I also write in the margins of my books with the vague notion that people, especially my kids, may someday want to read from my library and have the benefit of my commentary. Kirsten teases me about it and gently encourages me to donate more of my "wisdom" to Goodwill so that we can make some room on our overstuffed bookcases. I know she's only playing, but the fact is, I do long for my ideas to find a home in the hearts of others. It's important to me to know that I've shared the best of what I knew. It's why I wrote this book.

The other thing I hope they'll say about me when I'm gone is that I carried the torch for my family. I was given a solid running start in life, and I've tried to make good use of those advantages by paying them forward. If I can keep alive my grandfather's courage, my mother-in-law's altruism, and my great-grandmother's passion, I'll be satisfied that my life was not lived in vain. That's the lessons of three generations handed down.

We hang a lot of little signs around our house. Maxims to remind us of important truths. "Home is wherever you are." "Be the best you can be and have fun doing it." "Give those children roots and wings." Or my daughters' least favorite: "There's no such thing as being bored, only boring people." They roll their eyes, but I'm pretty sure they're going to recall where they heard it, and I hope it makes them smile when they do.

Who knows, though? Things get lost in translation. I may be erroneously attributed with having said, "It's better to be at the bottom of a ladder you want to climb than the top of one you don't." I used this idea in my TEDx Talk, and I credited *The Office* in the following breath. In spite of that, everyone from the rock band Daughtry to the Washington Speakers Bureau to bestselling author Chris Guillebeau has credited me with having made it up. There are items on Pinterest devoted to my having invented these words. I'm sure Ricky Gervais (the creator and lead writer of *The Office*) has bigger fish to fry than trying to set the record straight about who said it first, but part of me wonders if I may someday be most celebrated for having come up with an insight that wasn't my own.

We have little control over the way we are remembered beyond our best efforts. People will vary in their version of events and there's not much to be done about that. But the clearer and more consistent we are about representing what it is we value, and acting on those values, the greater chance we have of being commemorated for them. As Maya Angelou said, "When you learn, teach. When you get, give."

●⋯⋯⋯⋯⋯●⋯⋯⋯⋯●

Should we choose to ignore our legacy, the paradox is that, even then we have made a statement of noncommitment. There is no way to stay out of the conversation. Even in suicide, we cannot erase what we were. In fact, then the annihilation becomes the legacy alongside question marks and a shroud over what might have been.

It's staggering when you think about how much your own little life impacts the lives of everyone you come in contact with *and* some you do not. That can feel like a lot of burden to put on the day-to-day when we already have our hands full trying to keep up with the laundry and making sure the dog is fed. But in addition to the ripples we realize we are making, there are those that go unrealized. Every bit as important and even harder to direct, I call this *the unintended legacy*.

THE UNINTENDED LEGACY

When you die, what will they find tucked away in your closets and drawers? What unsolved mysteries will be revealed in your attic and basement? Old letters full of embarrassing personal details? A nude picture of a past lover? Lingerie you haven't worn in years but can't quite bring yourself to throw in the trash? A few unsmoked joints? A sex toy? A stash of candy bars? Or perhaps it's something more interesting that for some reason you didn't want anyone to know about, as was the case with Vivian Maier. She took 100,000 photos of street life during World War II, and they weren't discovered until her death in 2009. For the record, you'll find no such treasure trove in my attic.

And what relic that might have told a thousand tales will be glossed over and tossed without a second thought by whomever is in charge of cleaning out your belongings? Jack Roetter was my hero, but when he passed away, I only took two books, a suit, and a belt buckle to remember him by. Maybe that was for the best. What if I'd found something scandalous that undid my high opinion of him? Stuff like that happens all the time. We disguise facets of our personality as well as our transgressions because we don't want anyone's positive impressions of us tarnished.

On the flip side, what if there was something buried in the rubble that I was supposed to know about? A treatise on life, or a key to a safe deposit box that none of us were aware of. I guess we'll never know.

It makes sense that we worry about our secret stashes. We will not, after all, be available for comment or explanation. If anyone were to dig through my possessions, they would find in my journals some pretty unfiltered thoughts. Should I throw them out now and avoid potential awkwardness, or will my Daughters of the American Revolution Good Citizenship Award cancel out whatever crazy stuff I wrote on those pages? Depends on who reads them. Either way, those hidden aspects that are revealed when we expire are going to be a part of our unintended legacy.

•⋯⋯⋯⋯•⋯⋯⋯⋯•

When I watch my daughter Adeline dance, I'm floored by her drive and artistic authenticity. It brings tears to my eyes to see her floating across the stage like a hummingbird. And if her peers don't bring the same level of intensity, they'd better watch out—her self-expression is a serious business. People tell me she gets it from me, but it's not anything I am conscious of having cultivated. Her sister Noelle has the ability to walk into a room and see everyone in it as a potential friend. This clearly comes from Kirsten's side of the family (we already know that I'm afraid of strangers), but it's not something I believe was ever taught deliberately.

The same can be said of my temper. I carry the anger inside of me, and while I do my best to channel it into productive outlets, I bristle when I see my offspring overcome by that all-too-familiar emotion. Heaven help me if one of my kids ends up with a drinking problem. I'll never forgive myself. These are things I wouldn't knowingly pass on to my children, but nonetheless they're also a piece of the unintended legacy.

• ⋯⋯⋯⋯⋯ • ⋯⋯⋯⋯⋯ •

We may imagine that the more time we have, the bigger our chances of establishing a worthwhile legacy. While that's certainly possible, there are also decent odds that the longer we hang around, the more likely we are to screw it up. Look at Bill Cosby. What happened there? The guy appeared to have everything. He was "Mr. Jell-O Pudding Pop," the star of one of the most successful series in TV history, and a huge advocate for education and family values. Meanwhile, most of what we'll remember about him is that he also drugged and raped women. I'm sure this was not how he saw himself being immortalized when he was accepting his 54th Emmy Award.

Like a watchdog making sure we show up as our best selves, the unintended legacy extends in every direction. It's the butterfly flapping its wings; the idea that when you check the organ donor box at the DMV, you may save someone's life, but you'll never know. It all stems from a belief that we are interconnected, even if only in the slipstream of an algorithm, and therefore benefit from looking out for one another.

Do the people who have impacted our trajectory consciously or unconsciously know they have? I'm sure most do not. To the doctor who stepped in and treated my mom when she almost died giving birth to me; to the teacher who taught me my first guitar chord; to David Coverdale who sparked a dream in my young self; to each and every talent buyer who gave me a shot to share that dream—thank you. I don't know these people, and they don't know me, but I got to be a part of their legacy. Whether they realized it or not, they made a difference in my life. Now go live yours, but keep in mind you're leaving behind so much more than you could ever imagine. Give 'em something beautiful to remember you by.

PART THREE

AFTERWORD

wanted to put the Afterword at the beginning. Before the introduction. It wouldn't have made any sense, but I felt a strong urge to have some kind of disclaimer. Something to acknowledge that getting this all down was *way* more involved than I ever imagined. Needless to say, I developed a tremendous reverence for the authors of the world. Andy Rooney used to joke that everyone thinks they would write a book "if only they had the time." If you know someone who has actually pulled it off, regardless of size or quality, you should buy that person a coffee, or better yet, purchase their book.

As an avid reader myself, I recognize good writing when I see it. Throughout the process of birthing *Objects in the Mirror,* there were times I would wrestle with essays for months on end, to no avail. Like a 250-page song that never seemed to resolve, I found myself overwhelmed on more than one occasion. It's disheartening to work hard on something and not be quite satisfied. And yet, here we are at the end. It's time for me to let go. The origin of the word *perfect* comes from the Latin *perfectus,* which means "completed." And I'm as complete as I'm going to get with this experiment. When it's all said and done, you either agree or disagree with what I set down on paper in this modest volume.

I chose to write about marriage, friends, kids, parents, and heroes because they have been the central relationships in my own life. I picked time, health, a sense of humor, work, forgiveness, integrity, and the legacy we leave behind as the line items we should focus our energy on because they occur to me as the pillars that hold up my own soul. I may have failed to touch on some big important topics in here, and I'm sure once I've sent the final manuscript to the printer, it will occur to me what they were. Perhaps someday when I've recovered from the ordeal of being a first-time author, I'll write about those too.

One of the girls asked me just last night, "Dad, do you think you'll write another book?"

"I don't know, honey," I answered truthfully.

"I hope not," she said.

What I do know is this: I have told you the truth as I see it, and in attempting to convey these stories, I have learned more than I ever would have had I kept them all to myself. That's the medicine. As challenging as this has been, I'm grateful to have had the opportunity. I now look forward to drinking Dom Pérignon and holding the first copy in my hands. To being able to say that I made it through. More than any of that, I'm excited to have a bit of my life back, to not be skipping dinners with my family or sequestering myself for long periods of time while I sandblast my philosophies. Evaluating our beliefs is a great practice, but doing it every day for the better part of two years is not for the faint of heart. Now that I've said what I had to say, it's not really mine anymore. It's yours. I hope you felt it was worth your time.

Neil Gaiman says, "A book is a dream that you hold in your hands." I don't know whether he means a dream like the kind you have at night or a dream like the kind you have of who you're going to be when you grow up, but regardless, he was right about both.

Thanks for being a part of my dream.

— Stephen Kellogg
Summer 2019

ACKNOWLEDGMENTS

Books do not happen in a vacuum. There are many people to thank for the safe passage of these ideas into the world, but I'd like to start with some of the folks who jumped in early and said they'd buy any book I wrote. That means something.

Thank you Aaron Kraus, Adaline Kujala, Alana Nucera, Alyssa Love, Amelia Mayo, Amy Carmichael, Anna Sebourn, Barb Edelheit, Barbara Steinberg, Brayden McCullough, Brendan Egan, Brye Blayne, Chad and Kara, Chip Burton, Christian Bello, Colleen Weiler, Courtney Knox, Daniel Poposki, the Deutch Family, Diane Davis, Elizabeth Glotch, Emily Holman, Eugene Slesicki, Glen Peer, James Mershon, Jason and Sarah Rylick, Jason Smith, Jay Miolla (evil twin brother), Jay Shapiro, Jen Dorner, Jennie Sue Olson, Julie Fancy, Julie Murphy Agnew, Karyn McQueen, Kerrie DiMarino, Kerry Anne Smith, Kimberly Boggs, Lane Beaumont, Laura Weigold, Leanne Krueger, Lee Lunt, Lou Sommer,

Mallori Openchowski, Marissa Skaggs, Marlena Purchiar-
oni, Matthew Debelak, Matthew Dunn, Meg Allwein,
Meghan Haenn, Melissa Fitts, Michael Jones, Michele
Carlson, Mike Ritschdorff, Mike Sabetta, Noah Jellison,
Patty Merola, Rachel Hawkins, Raegan Cury, Rebecca
Farley-Dimino, Rich and Laura Shaw, Rich Bodnar, Richard
Catalano, Ron and Deb Kepnach, Sarah McGinnis, Scott
Jerome, Steven Taylor, Thomas Shappley, Tiffany Erickson,
Tina Stroud, and Vikki Evans.

Next, I'd like to recognize my editor, Carol Stanley, for
gently but firmly guiding me through this process. Your suggestions were not only a great asset to my writing but also to
my thinking. From our first meeting at Musso & Frank's, I
knew I trusted you—you've been a great friend.

To my copyeditor, Lindsay Bender: Thanks for maintaining my tone of voice throughout the manuscript and accepting my premise that *sometimes proper grammar is for suckers.*

To Lisa Duff, James Campion, Don Miggs, and Andrew
Oxton: Your initial suggestions about the direction of the
book helped shape something I was excited to write about.

To Jeff Goins, Josh Ritter, and Dan Gemeinhart: You set the bar high.

To Ed Caffrey: You gave me a sanctuary to write in when the world got too noisy.

To the characters in this book: You inspired me and allowed me, however unwittingly, to share your story as well.

To my early readers, Josh Friend, Kenny Corbett, Dave Chalfant, Sara Mahoney, Kirsten Kellogg, Shady Katz, and Eric Donnelly: Without your feedback, I would have been sunk. I owe you all a debt of gratitude.

To my manager and most avid reader, Jessica K. Martin: Without you I could never have pulled *this* rabbit out of *this* hat. Thanks for always making time for my calls and caring deeply about what was being written. In many ways we share a brain, even more so now.

To my friends and family who saw less of me over the last two years than I would have liked: Your patience and encouragement traveled with me everywhere I went. There are so many things to be grateful for, most of all you.

PHOTOGRAPHY CREDITS

OBJECTS IN THE MIRROR: THOUGHTS ON A PERFECT LIFE FROM AN IMPERFECT PERSON DISCUSSION QUESTIONS

1. *Objects in the Mirror* outlines 12 pillars to a life well lived. If you had to pick from the book the three areas in your own life that are the most important, which would you choose? Is there another pillar, not listed in the book, that you would add to your story?

2. At the beginning of the chapter on marriage, Stephen recounts an argument with his wife where he asks her if she thinks he's "a dick or just acting like a dick?" Can you recall a time when you "acted like a dick" in one of your own relationships? Were you able to resolve the conflict? If so, how?

3. In the chapter on friendship, there is an exploration of how the advent of social media has altered the way we interact with one another. Do you agree? Can you think of instances where social media has been beneficial to your relationships?

4. Whether you yourself have kids or not, how has becoming an adult changed your perspective of your own childhood? What

things are you most grateful for about the way that you were treated as a young person? Were there aspects you resent? If so, how can you improve those things for the children in your own life?

5. One of the possible takeaways from the chapter on parents is that, while we may be justified in criticizing our parents, we are also responsible for what we do with our respective upbringing. Do you agree? What was the best thing that you learned from your parents? If you're a parent yourself, how has your feeling about the way you were raised shifted since becoming one?

6. Recount a time when you found out that a hero of yours was not exactly who you thought they were. Do we hold ourselves to the same standards we use to judge celebrities and those we idolize?

7. In a world that can often feel like it's consistently speeding up, time may be the greatest commodity we have. Ideally, how would you prioritize yours? As a follow up, how close is your current use of time to that ideal? If you find that it's not very close, is there anything you can do to improve that?

8. With our understanding of health evolving on an almost daily basis, it can be tricky to know exactly what the best course of action is. Stephen highlights food, exercise, regular doctor visits, attention to the spirit, and rest as the areas he focuses

on with regard to his health. Share what has worked best for you in your own life.

9. What is the best job you've ever had? What's the worst? After reading the chapter on work, is there anything you think you might have been able to do differently in the less-than-stellar jobs that might have made them more fulfilling?

10. On a scale of 1 to 10, how good is your sense of humor? Recall a time when your sense of humor was the "invaluable friend you didn't know you had."

11. The first sentence in the chapter on integrity is, "The truth is never a bad idea." Do you agree? Defend your answer.

12. Share a time when you needed to forgive someone but it wasn't easy. Now share a time when you yourself needed to be forgiven. The idea that holding a grudge is a poison to the soul and that forgiveness is its own reward pervades this chapter. Have you withheld your forgiveness? Is there someone you could make it right with by trying?

13. The chapter on legacy states that *you matter* and your legacy is the reason why. What kind of legacy do you hope to leave behind? Are there aspects of the unintended legacy that you suspect will be left in your wake? Do you find the idea of a legacy comforting or intimidating?

PRAISE FOR THE ALBUM
OBJECTS IN THE MIRROR

"...a snapshot of American life in 2018—raw, hopeful, and honest."
—Noisetrade

"Objects in the Mirror *captures the talent, spontaneity, and humanity of Kellogg's songwriting...refreshingly free of pretense and studio polishing...like John Prine fronting The Heartbreakers...Kellogg's relaxed vocal delivery and just enough pedal steel and piano strike the sonic sweet spot."*
—Rolling Stone

"...inviting heartland Rock N' Roll sound with a view that seems to suggest that happiness is all about perspective."
—Twangville

"With beautifully written songs and an engaging personality, Kellogg appears as if he was born on stage, taking the spotlight and using it to his advantage, but never letting go of his connection with the audience."
—Michigan Daily

"...we are reminded of how touching Kellogg's songs are, never more so than on his latest, the blindingly beautiful Objects in the Mirror."
—Planet Bluegrass

For information on live events, other albums, and merchandise, visit StephenKellogg.com

 Stephen_Kellogg

@Stephen_Kellogg

 @StephenKelloggMusic